P9-CDX-550

The Fifth Harmonic

The Fifth Harmonic

a novel

F. PAUL WILSON

HAMPTON ROADS
PUBLISHING COMPANY, INC.

Cover design by Marjoram Productions
Cover art © 2003 Digital Vision/PictureQuest;
Corbis Images/PictureQuest; Brand X Pictures/Alamy;
Image 100/Alamy; www.comstock.com

Hampton Roads Publishing Company, Inc.
1125 Stoney Ridge Road
Charlottesville, VA 22902

434-296-2772
fax: 434-296-5096
e-mail: hrpc@hrpub.com
www.hrpub.com

If you are unable to order this book from your local
bookseller, you may order directly from the publisher.
Call 1-800-766-8009, toll-free.

Library of Congress Cataloging-in-Publication Data
Wilson, F. Paul (Francis Paul)
The fifth harmonic : a novel / F. Paul Wilson.
    p. cm.
ISBN 1-57174-386-3 (alk. paper)
1. Throat--Cancer--Patients--Fiction. 2. Physicians--Fiction. I.
Title.
 PS3573.I45695F54 2003
 813'.54--dc22
                                        2003014796

ISBN 1-57174-386-3

10 9 8 7 6 5 4 3 2 1

Printed on acid-free paper in the United States

Author's Note

The author wishes to acknowledge the work of Ronald Wright and Charles Gallenkamp for taking him places he could not go himself.

PART ONE

The Shining Blind Man
in the Fortress

1

Katonah, NY

Not much doing in this quaint little Westchester town on a hot Thursday afternoon, so Will felt free to crawl his Land Rover past the brick- and clapboard-fronted shops on the tree-lined main drag as he scanned their windows: a café, an optician, Hallmark cards, one-hour photo—

There. Black letters on a plate-glass window: HEALER. No wonder he'd missed them on his first pass; they couldn't be more than two inches tall, barely visible from the street.

He spotted an empty parking space right in front and eased into it. He turned off the engine but left the keys in the ignition. He still wasn't sure he could do this.

With the air conditioning off, the Rover's interior began to bake in the late August sun. Still he sat staring at the tiny storefront. Nothing terribly threatening about the exterior. In fact he couldn't imagine how it could be more low-keyed. A curtain of some sort of red-and-white embroidered fabric stretched across the lower three quarters of the window, high enough to keep all but the Patrick Ewings of the world from seeing inside. The word HEALER sat off-center to the left, toward the solid white door with the dripping air conditioner in its transom.

And that was it. No come-ons, no promises. Just . . . HEALER.

The only visible clue as to what the place might be about were the many-colored crystals hanging from threads above the curtain.

I must be crazy, he thought. How can I go in there?

He peered up and down the shady sidewalk, scanning for pedestrians. A young woman pushing a baby carriage off to his left, heading away, otherwise all quiet here on the fringe of a commercial district that looked frozen in 1947. Lunch time had passed, and it was way too hot to be out window shopping.

Good. Less chance of being spotted if he did decide to go in. Will lived over in Bedford and had his internal medicine practice there, but a fair number of his patients lived in Katonah. He didn't want any of them spotting him going into a place like this.

But then, why the hell should he care? Especially now that he didn't have a practice anymore.

Though the question was rhetorical, the answer flared in his mind: Because it went against everything he believed in, because he had nothing but contempt for these people, these so-called psychic healers, these phonies, these charlatans, these "new-age" leeches who attached themselves to sick, desperate people and sucked off their money with empty promises of miracle cures.

His knuckles whitened as his hands squeezed the leather-wrapped steering wheel. He forced himself to loosen his grip. Lighten up.

At least when I go in, he thought, it will be with my eyes open.

If I go in.

Do it, he told himself. What have you got to lose?

Nothing but my self-respect.

He sighed. Yeah . . . his self-respect. And what would that mean three months from now?

As they say, desperate times called for desperate measures.

Will grabbed the baseball cap from where it lay on the passenger seat and jammed it onto his head. He checked in the mirror to make sure the turtleneck collar hid the angry red scar on his throat.

A turtleneck in August, he thought; she's going to think I need a shrink.

He caught a glimpse of his blue eyes and the new wrinkles around them . . . worry lines, someone might call them. Well, that same someone could say he'd had some stress lately. And maybe that had shaken a little more salt into his predominately pepper-colored hair. He noticed that his normally full-cheeked face looked pale and drawn. For the first time in his forty-nine years, Will looked his age.

He pulled the hat brim low, yanked the keys from the ignition, and stepped out into the heat. Feeling like a fugitive, he glanced up and down the sidewalk again—empty. Six quick, long strides and three heartbeats later he'd reached the door and was stepping through into the cool interior.

A bell on the door jangled as he closed it behind him.

If she's psychic, why does she need a doorbell?

Then again, where does it say she's psychic?

Nowhere.

Be fair.

He stared around, letting his eyes adjust to the lower light. A small, unadorned room, done in beige and brown, with minimal furnishings—a single desk, a table with some magazines atop and two chairs tucked against it—all of it looking secondhand. A beaded curtain hung across a doorway at the rear. Tiny open flames danced everywhere—candles of every size, shape, and shade sat on every available horizontal surface, glowed from multiple sconces on the walls.

The rest of the light came through the windows, filtered through crystals. Of course . . . couldn't do the new age thing without crystals. They hung on threads inside the big front window, cluttered the sills of the small, high, side windows—amethysts, rose quartz, carnelians, aquamarines—throwing rainbows about the room.

Despite all his apprehensions, Will felt himself begin to relax. The candles and the crystalline light had a soothing, comforting effect.

Lulling was probably a more accurate description. He was sure the room hadn't been set up this way by chance.

And yet . . . he sensed a sort of temporariness about the place, as if this were just one stop on a long journey, that everything here could be left behind at a moment's notice.

He heard noise at the rear, then a woman stepped through the beaded doorway. Will was immediately struck by her looks. Her long dark hair—black, really . . . black as the deepest cellar of a cavern—was gathered behind her neck and held by an embroidered band. Smooth mocha skin stretched across a strong jaw and high cheekbones. But it was her eyes—the jade green of her irises stabbed out from her dark face and pinned him against the door.

She smiled without showing her teeth.

"Yes? Can I help you?"

He swallowed—where had all his saliva gone?—and removed his cap.

"Yes," he managed. "I want . . . do you do consultations?"

"About your health? Yes, if you wish," her voice rich and throaty, with a strange accent, as if she'd learned English in Seville . . . from a Parisian.

Her eyes released him as she moved toward the desk, and Will saw that she was barefoot. He took in the rest of her. Five-five, five-six, maybe, wearing a loose white blouse and khaki slacks. Her broad shoulders and straight-backed, almost military posture gave her body an angular look. He liked her looks, her understated clothes. Under different circumstances he might be thinking of ways to get to know her.

From the street he'd spotted what looked like an apartment on the second floor. He wondered if she lived there.

She opened a desk drawer, pulled out an index card, and slid it across to him. He noticed that her fingers were long and her nails were short, unnibbled, and unpainted. How many sets of unpainted fingernails in Westchester County, he wondered.

"Please write your name and address for me."

Will moved away from the door and took the chair on the near side of the desk. He pulled out a pen . . . and hesitated. How much should he give away?

As little as possible.

But he wouldn't lie. He wrote "W. C. Burleigh" but left off the M.D., and gave the address of his now empty office. He glanced up at her.

"Do—don't you want any past medical history?"

"I will get to that. I have my own way of taking one." Her green eyes narrowed, concentrating their agate light until it seemed to pierce his skin and look right through him. "You seem very tense."

Oh, there's a real diagnostic coup, he thought. A kindergartner could see I'm just about ready to jump out of my skin.

Yet he had to admit that this was a woman with extraordinary presence. She seemed to fill the room. Which was certainly an asset in the charlatan trade.

"I am," he said. Might as well get it out in the open. "You can't imagine how uncomfortable I am being here."

"Really? Why?"

"Because I don't believe in any of this . . ." He'd almost said "shit" but bit it back and let the sentence hang.

She surprised him by smiling, showing white, even teeth this time. Close up now he noticed how her smile created little dimple-like creases around the corners of her mouth.

"I have wondered why I was sent to Westchester County. Sometimes I think it was to make believers out of people like you."

"Sent?"

"Perhaps 'sent' is too strong. *Guided.*"

"By whom?"

"Just . . . guided. But if you 'don't believe in any of this,' and being here makes you so uncomfortable, why did you come?"

"Because I'm sick."

Her smile faded. "I know."

Did she? Did she really? Or was that simply a logical conclusion about a man in a place with "HEALER" on the front window?

No way she could know *how* sick.

"Tell me about it," she said.

"I'd rather you tell *me*. About it, that is."

"You have already seen your regular doctor, I assume?"

"Yes. A number of them."

"And?"

"They tell me I'm sick."

Will spoke the words softly, struggling to keep his tone neutral. He didn't want to sound belligerent, but he wanted to give away as little as possible. He'd read about psychics and palm readers and such, and how they were adept at wheedling information out of unsuspecting marks. She wasn't getting any freebies from him.

"And now you come to me. To . . . what? Test me?"

Was that amusement or annoyance in her eyes? He couldn't be sure. Either way, it unsettled him.

"No . . . I don't know. I spoke to Savanna Walters."

A smile again, warm this time. "Ah, Savanna. A sweet woman."

Yes, Savanna was that—in spades. An independent, delightfully witty spinster who had been one of Will's first patients when he'd hung out his *Internal Medicine* shingle nearly two decades ago. He'd guided her through a number of minor illnesses and one serious, stubborn case of pneumonia. But when he'd investigated some abnormalities in her blood count last year, and a bone marrow aspiration confirmed the diagnosis of acute lymphocytic leukemia, he knew he was out of his depth. He'd sent her to an oncologist-hematologist, and figured he'd never see Savanna again: the prognosis for ALL in her age group was extremely grim.

Then last week, on his next-to-last day in the office, she'd shocked him by showing up looking fit and healthy. She said she'd heard he was sick and closing his practice. Actually he'd sold the practice to the local hospital; they'd made a preemptive offer of half a million to cut out the Manhattan medical centers that had been gobbling up private practices all over Westchester County. The hospital had two young doctors lined up to take over—*two* men to handle what he'd been doing solo.

Leaving the practice was the hardest thing he'd ever done in his life. The breakup of his marriage couldn't hold a candle to the pain he'd felt when he closed the door behind him that last day.

"Savanna," he said. "You're . . ."

"Alive?" she said, eyes twinkling. "Yes. I'm cured."

"That's wonderful! But Dr. Singh told me you'd stopped treatment."

"Only with him. After one chemotherapy session, I knew it wasn't for me. So I found somebody else."

"He must be a miracle worker."

"Yes. *She* is." Savanna reached into her purse and pulled out a slip of paper. She pressed it into his hand. "This is her address. See her. Please. She helped cure me. She can do the same for you."

"Cured your leukemia?" Will said, baffled. "How?"

"She worked with me and together we killed it."

What a strange way to put it. *We killed it*—not cured it . . . killed it.

"She can help you kill yours. She has ways," Savanna said, as if that explained it all.

"Oh, well," he said, not knowing quite how to respond. He supposed word had got out about his malignancy, but it seemed so bizarre to have a patient refer him for treatment. "I don't think . . ."

"She cured me, Dr. Burleigh. Maybe she can cure you." Her bright blue eyes begged him. "Please go see her. Please."

After Savanna left, Will called her oncologist who was flabbergasted that Savanna was still alive. Singh confirmed that she'd had her first dose of chemotherapy and never returned for the rest, never returned his staff's repeated calls to her home.

The oncologist guessed that Savanna had had a spontaneous remission—extremely rare in ALL, but it happened. Will agreed. A spontaneous remission. What else could it be?

But over the next few days Savanna's words haunted him: *She cured me, Dr. Burleigh. Maybe she can cure you. Please go see her. Please.*

And now, against all reason, against all common sense, here he was.

"How is Savanna?" she said.

"Fine, as far as I can tell. She told me you cured her leukemia."

"I am glad she's doing well."

That wasn't what he was looking for. "Did you?" he said. "Cure her?"

"No."

Her answer startled him. Here was a perfect opportunity to take credit for Savanna's spontaneous remission—he'd handed it to her on the proverbial silver platter—and she was denying it.

"But she says you did."

"That is very generous of Savanna, but I merely helped her toward a cure."

This wasn't going the way Will had expected. Why was she dodging credit? Why so evasive? Does she think I'm with the Department of Health or Consumer Affairs?

Or is she mimicking me?

Either way, he wanted to bring this to a head.

"All right then: Can you help me the same way?"

"I can try."

Frustration nibbled at him. She wasn't following his imagined script: No promises of a cure, and she hadn't even mentioned money. She was acting very professional. And that bothered him.

"And the cost?"

He had expected nothing from this encounter beyond satisfying his curiosity, and was willing to pay for that—up to a point. But he didn't want to be ripped off for some ungodly sum.

"Let us first see if I can help you. Come this way."

No money down. All right, so maybe she wasn't a bunco artist. Maybe she was just another delusional character who thought she had a direct line to the secrets of the universe. Her kind, despite their sincerity, were still almost as dangerous as the larcenous phony if they kept sick people away from proven therapy.

Then why the hell am I here?

Because you're a coward, he heard a voice say in his head. Because you can't face the proven therapy for what you've got.

She stepped through the beaded curtain and held it aside for him. He followed her through the doorway and down a narrow, curved set of stairs to another candlelit room in the basement. No windows here, however, and hence no rainbows dancing around the room. A pair of oak chairs and a small oak table, similar in provenance to the ones upstairs, were the only furniture. On the table, four oddly shaped metal objects, each a different color, were arranged on a white cloth. But the feature that grabbed Will's attention was the large rectangular opening cut into the concrete slab of the basement floor. It looked to be about four by eight feet, and was filled with sand.

Westchester County seemed light years away.

"Remove your shoes and lie down, please," she said, pointing to the opening.

"In there?"

"Yes. On the sand."

"Why?"

"Because I wish you to be in contact with the earth."

Curiouser and curiouser, he thought as he sat on one of the chairs and pulled off his loafers and socks. I must be more desperate than I imagined.

He padded across the cool concrete of the floor to the makeshift sandbox, but paused on the edge like a hesitant swimmer contemplating a cold pool. Did she really mean for him to . . . ?

"You did say to lie down."

"Yes, I did."

She didn't look at him; she was intent on her metal things, handling them one at a time. Each ran about eight inches long, slim and cylindrical at one end, flaring and flattening to a rough, wavy triangular shape at the other.

"Flat on your back, please. Don't worry. It's dry. You won't catch a cold."

A cold is the least of my worries, he thought.

Feeling slightly ridiculous, he stepped onto the cool granular bed and stretched out. As the back of his head came to rest on the sand, he realized he'd reap an extra benefit from the turtleneck shirt: no sand down his collar.

"How does it feel?" she said, stepping closer and looking down at him.

"Sandy."

A flicker of a smile, and he realized he was pleased he could make her smile. He wanted to dislike her, distrust her—bunco or bonkers, either way she could cause harm to the wrong person—but found himself responding to, and envying, her aura of serenity.

Aura . . . listen to me. Been here ten minutes and already I'm starting to sound new-agey myself.

"Press your heels and your palms into the sand. That's your Mother you're feeling."

"My mother died five years ago."

"No, I mean the Mother of us all. The earth."

Oh, boy, he thought. Here it comes.

"It is one of the tragedies of modern living that we never touch her. Industrial society has cut off its inhabitants from the living world. You live and work in structures made of dead material, travel enclosed in rubber and steel, and even when you stroll through the pockets of living things you call 'parks,' it is with your feet encased in rubber sneakers treading macadam paths. Think: when was the last time your body was in contact with the earth—when was the last time even the soles of your *shoes* touched her soil? Why do you see people lined up in their cars like steel lemmings heading for the beaches? It is the only time all year they actually touch their Mother. They come away feeling renewed after merely brushing her hem."

"Ooookay," Will said, wriggling his hands and feet into the sand. This woman might be beautiful but he feared her antenna was picking up the wrong channels. "There. I'm dug in."

"Good. How does it feel?"

"Really good," he said. He was tempted to add, *Just like sand in a hole in the floor of somebody's basement,* but didn't want to trigger another lecture.

"See? That is your Mother."

He thought, I know who my mother is—was—and it's not a handful of sand.

Holding one of her metal things by its cylindrical end, she stepped onto the sand and squatted next to him.

"What's that?"

"This?" She held it up, twisting it back and forth, letting ruddy light reflect from the flared end. She plucked the tip and it gave off a faint musical note. "This is one of the four tines."

"What's it for?"

"I am going to survey your *chakras.*"

"My what?"

"Your chakras—the energy centers of your body. Chakra is the Sanskrit word for wheel. Each of us has seven energy centers in our body."

Only seven? he wanted to say. We have zillions. They're called *cells*. But he kept mum.

"I will check the first now."

She held the tine over his groin, about two inches above the fly of his tan Dockers, and began moving it in clockwise circles.

"What's this telling you?" he said, a little uncomfortable with the area of her attention.

"Other than the fact that there is no woman in your life right now," she said, utterly deadpan, "all is well here."

Damn. She was right. Pretty risky for her to say that with nothing to go on. True, he wasn't wearing his wedding ring—he'd stopped after the divorce—but she could have found herself way out on a limb with that little declaration. In fact . . .

"What if I told you that I have been deeply involved with a woman for the past two years?"

"I would not believe you."

"You can be that sure?"

"Not completely, but I can tell you that if such a woman exists, you are not having sexual relations with her. Your first chakra is very congested."

Embarrassed, Will opened his mouth to make some sort of excuse but she cut him off.

"Please. Let me complete my survey and we can talk afterwards. I do not wish to be distracted."

She now began rotating the tine over his lower abdomen. Once she seemed satisfied there, she switched to another tine, this with golden highlights, plucked it, and rotated it over his solar plexus. After a short stay there, she glided it up to his heart. A moment or two later, she gave a faint nod. No problem there, apparently.

Will held his breath as she plucked the tine that gave off greenish hues and brought it toward his throat. This is it, lady. This is where you blow it.

She poised the tine over his turtleneck collar, then—

"Oh!"

She blinked and snatched her hand back; he felt the tine drop against his throat.

"What's the matter?" he said, feeling an uneasy chill dance up his spine. Had she really sensed something?

"Wait," she said. "Just give me a minute."

She retrieved the tine and again poised it over his throat. He couldn't see the metal but he thought he heard its hum change in pitch. He watched her troubled expression. Finally she rose and turned away.

"Your fifth chakra—your throat—you are very ill."

Will lay still a moment. How did she know? How *could* she know?

"What's wrong?" he said, trying to sound calm, hiding his agitation by pushing himself to his feet and brushing the sand off his clothes.

"There is a traitor in your fifth chakra. Mutiny." She turned to him now, pain in her eyes. "You need to see a doctor."

"I have. I've had all the necessary tests." He pulled down the turtleneck collar to reveal the two-inch scar on the right side of his throat. "Even a lymph node biopsy."

"What did they find?"

"A very aggressive tumor at the base of my tongue; it's already begun to infiltrate my larynx—my voice box."

"Yes, I know."

Will felt a hot blast of anger—Like hell you do!—but it cooled quickly as he remembered what she'd said a moment ago: *There is a traitor in your fifth chakra. Mutiny.* She was right. What else was a tumor but a traitor—a cluster of his own cells that had gone mutinous and turned against him?

"Can you help me?" he said.

She shook her head. "You must see a specialist. I can recommend some."

That floored him. She was sending him away—referring him. A bitter laugh rose in his throat.

"Been there, done that," he said. "I've been to the best."

"It is incurable?"

"No. It's curable. But the cure is unacceptable."

"What—?"

"I don't want to go into all that now. All I want to know is if you can do for me what you did for Savanna."

Or what Savanna *thinks* you did for her.

How pathetic. Am I so desperate that I'll stoop to humoring a new-age nutcase on the outside chance that some sort of miracle lightning will strike?

Yes. He was that desperate. Because he had no other options, nowhere else to go.

"I don't know," she said slowly. "It is possible, but it will be especially difficult with one such as you."

"What's that mean?"

"You are closed off—you are one of the most closed-off people I have ever met."

I'll take that as a compliment, he thought. He seated himself and began slipping back into his socks and shoes.

"You must be open if I am to help you. I must think on this. May I get back to you?"

Will wasn't sure if he should feel disappointed that she was putting him off, or elated because he didn't have to decide right here and now whether or not to commit to a course of hocus-pocus medicine.

"Sure. But don't wait too long. One thing I don't have a lot of is time."

"How long do you have?"

Will felt his throat constrict. "Well, if I don't go for the surgery and the umpteen radiation treatments it'll take to kill this thing— and I'm doing neither—they tell me that I've definitely seen my last Christmas tree. Maybe even my last Thanksgiving turkey."

Will saw her shudder. He wondered how he'd looked when he first heard the news. He found himself still unable to accept the fact that the remaining months of his life could be numbered on one hand.

"Come upstairs," she said.

He followed her back up to the front room. Her step seemed heavier than before, almost weary. She stopped by the desk and picked up his index card.

"'W. C. Burleigh.' Is that what they call you—W. C.?"

"You mean, like W. C. Fields? No. I go by Will."

"Very well, Will. Can you leave me a phone number where I can reach you?"

He gave her his home phone and she jotted it down. Then she stepped to the door and held it open for him.

"I will call you tomorrow night."

"What's going to change between now and then?" he said, slipping the cap back onto his head.

"I must do some . . . research."

Research what? My Dun & Bradstreet?

Stop being such a cynical bastard.

"I'll be waiting for your call," he said as the blinding wet heat from the sidewalk slapped him. "By the way, what's *your* name?"

"Call me Maya," she said.

2

Bedford, NY

Will was sitting in the claustrophobic, chart-strewn dictation room of the hospital record department, signing off on the last of his open charts when Dave Andros popped in.

Just the man Will did *not* want to see.

"Hey, Will." Andros, a short, portly bundle of energy, dropped into the chair next to Will and fixed him with his dark eyes. "How're you feeling?"

"Decent."

He lifted Will's chin. "Let me see that incision." Dave leaned close, tilting his head left and right, then nodded. "Damn, I do good work!"

Will laughed. "You do, Dave."

"Yeah, I know." He continued to stare at Will. "Well?"

"Well what?"

"What's the final word from Sloane?"

"You didn't get a report?"

"Not yet. What did they think?"

Will sighed. "Same as everybody else."

Will had first noticed the lump in his neck a month ago while shaving: a firm, non-tender, subcutaneous mass about the size of the last phalanx of his little finger. No question—an enlarged lymph node. He'd watched it for about a week, fully expecting it to return to normal size.

Lymphomas, after all, happened to other people.

But the node did not shrink. In fact, Will suspected that it might be enlarging. And was that a second node he felt beneath it?

Uneasy now, he copped a hallway ENT consult from Dave, who said the fastest way to find out what was going on was to biopsy the node. And not to worry too much—even if it was a lymphoma, they were getting fabulous results these days.

Two days later, Dave removed the node under local in the outpatient surgical suite and sent it down to pathology for a quick read. As soon as the incision was sutured closed, Will headed for the path department where the frozen section results would be waiting for him.

He rapped on the door frame of Alex Reed's office. "What's the word, Alex?"

Reed was the hospital's chief pathologist. He was pushing sixty and his build mimicked his name; he sat folded in his chair, wrapped in a white lab coat with sleeves that were inches too short for him. He didn't smile when he looked up from his desk.

"Oh, Will. Have a seat. And close the door, will you?"

Something in the pathologist's eyes started a cold, sick dread growing in Will's gut. He closed the door but remained standing.

"What is it, Alex? Non-Hodgkin's lymphoma?"

"No. It's squamous, Will. The node was packed with squamous cell carcinoma."

"Oh, shit." Will's knees suddenly felt rubbery. He lowered himself into the chair. "You're sure?"

"Very. I'll be able to give you more details after I examine a full prep, but even in the frozen sections this appears to be one very aggressive-looking tumor. I suggest you get rolling on therapy right away."

"But where the hell's the primary?"

"Could be anywhere in the head or neck. You want my guess? I'd say the tongue."

Stunned, Will had stumbled out of Reed's office in search of Dave.

No more hallway consults now. Dave had Will come to his office where he did a thorough oral exam. He found what he thought might be the primary tumor far back at the base of Will's tongue.

"No symptoms?" Dave said. He looked a little gray; they'd been friends a long time. "No difficulty swallowing or a feeling of fullness back there?"

"No," Will told him. "Not a thing."

"They can be sneaky."

Will leaned back and closed his eyes. He felt as if the walls were caving in on him.

"Why, Dave?

"You don't smoke, do you?"

He knew where Dave was going: the major causes of oral cancers were smoke and alcohol.

"Quit cigarettes in medical school, although I smoked a pipe for awhile afterward, and I still have an occasional cigar."

Dave shook his head. "What asshole is responsible for bringing that foul habit back into vogue? How about booze?"

"Some red wine with dinner. Other than that . . ."

Why me? Will thought.

He'd seen hundreds of patients ask the same question. Usually the answer was obvious: they smoked too much, drank too much, had a family history that they'd ignored. But sometimes tumors simply happened. Will had taken decent care of himself over the years . . . this didn't seem fair.

He straightened and looked at Dave. No use miring himself in pity. He needed to attack this thing right away.

"Okay," he said. "What am I looking at for treatment?"

"Radiation and surgery," Dave said.

Will felt his intestines writhe at the words. "How much surgery?"

"I'd like to see an MRI before I answer that."

The final path report was ready the next day, and it confirmed Reed's initial impression: an aggressive squamous cell Ca. The MRI brought worse news: the tumor was already infiltrating around the larynx.

A very distressed Dave Andros had then told Will what he would have to do to save his life.

Will had recoiled, unable to accept what he'd heard. At Dave's urging he took the tissue slides and the MR films out for a second opinion. The matter of where was a no-brainer: Memorial Sloane-Kettering in nearby Manhattan had an international reputation.

"They said the same thing you did, Dave, only some of them want to toss in a little chemo for good measure."

Dave shook his head. "I wish there was another way, Will." He paused, then, "When are you going in?"

Will had been dreading this moment. Last week, while driving back from his consultation with the Sloane-Kettering team, he'd come to a gut-wrenching decision. During the ensuing days he'd reconsidered it from all angles, but the decision held. Since then he'd been avoiding Dave. He knew his old friend cared about him, knew how he'd react.

Bracing himself, Will took a deep breath and said, "I'm not."

Dave's eyes widened. "What do you mean?"

"Just what I said: no surgery, no radiation, no chemo. Nada."

Dave shot out of his chair and began pacing, which wasn't easy, considering the confined quarters of the dictation room.

"You can't be serious! You won't last three months!"

"Probably not. But it's better than living years with what I'll have left after the surgeons and radiologists get through with me—all without a guarantee that I'll be tumor free."

"But you'll die horribly, Will! It's a flip of the coin whether the tumor will close off your larynx or your esophagus first. If you don't choke to death, you'll die of starvation and dehydration."

Will stared at him. "No, I won't."

Dave stopped his pacing. "Oh, great! Just great! You think you're going to do a Kevorkian on yourself? What's it going to be? Morphine overdose? KCl? A .357 Magnum?"

Will hadn't chosen a method yet. He hadn't reached that point in his planning.

"Let's just say I won't die of starvation and dehydration."

Dave sat again and placed a hand on Will's arm. "You're not thinking straight, Will. I know it's scary, but you can't run from this. You've got to face it down and conquer it." He squeezed Will's arm. "The alternative is to sit and let the tumor rot you from the inside."

"I'm not going to sit. I'm going to travel—tumor and all—and go all those places I put off seeing while I figured I still had a long road ahead of me."

With a heavy heart, Will closed the chart before him and rose to his feet. He didn't want to argue with Dave, didn't want to see the anguish in his friend's eyes.

"And here's some words of wisdom from a man whose days are numbered: Enjoy life *now*, Dave. Do the things you want to do *now*. Don't put them off till later—sometimes later doesn't come."

He left Dave sitting in the chart room, staring at the floor.

Will stifled a belch as he walked toward the door of his two-story faux Tudor townhouse in Mount Kisco. He'd started renting it when he and Annie separated, and wound up staying on after the divorce. It wasn't fancy, but he didn't need fancy. He needed functional. This place was situated halfway between his office and the hospital. Mostly he just slept here.

He rubbed his abdomen. He felt a little bloated. He'd overeaten again at Armondo's Place, a dinner of steak au poivre, asparagus hollandaise, twice-baked potato, and German chocolate layer cake. He figured since he no longer had to worry about the long-term effects of saturated fats, he might as well indulge in a heavy meal whenever possible.

Too soon he'd be reduced to a liquid diet.

He was inside and halfway down the hall when he heard a knock. He opened the door and found his ex-wife standing there.

"Annie. What—?"

She stepped past him. "Dave Andros called me this afternoon."

"Oh, hell."

He closed the door and faced her. Annie was as attractive as ever, looking considerably younger than her forty-eight years, although she appeared slightly disheveled tonight. Her chestnut hair wasn't perfectly brushed, and the whites of her large brown eyes looked red. Had she been crying?

"'Oh, hell' is right," she said.

"He had no right—"

"Let's not get sidetracked on the patient privilege issue. Dave is your friend and he's worried about you. So am I, now that I know. I've been sitting out there in the parking lot for hours, waiting for you to come home."

He was touched. "You didn't have to."

"I'm hoping I can talk some sense into you."

Will gave her a smile. "You never could when we were married."

"But maybe I can now that we're not. I still care about you, Will. You know that."

He did know that. The breakup of their marriage had been his fault. Not because of a woman, but because of another kind of mistress, a very demanding one: his practice. He hadn't been a bad father to their only daughter, but as far as husbands go, he'd been mostly absent; Annie had needed more of a presence than he could provide.

The practice . . . the damn practice. He'd known he was obsessive about it—a solo practitioner had to be. That was why hardly anyone was solo anymore. He was a dinosaur and he knew it. Not that he hadn't tried to take in a partner over the years. Tried three times. They were all good docs, but somehow they just didn't have quite the zeal he was looking for. Hell, they all wanted a weekday off. What was that about? When was the last time he'd had a week*end* off, let alone a week*day*.

Maybe he was too scrupulous. Maybe he hadn't been able to relinquish the exacting control he imposed on his practice. You couldn't delegate responsibility in a group practice, but at some point you had to delegate authority. Will had been unable to do that. He needed to keep his finger on all the buttons. My way or the highway. That was why it had taken over his life.

That was why he was divorced and still in love with his wife. He'd let her take the house and just about anything else she wanted. All he'd kept were his old vinyl records from the sixties and his collection of western videos.

Annie was now engaged to a real estate broker whose business seemed to run itself. He had lots of time for Annie.

But somehow Will and Annie had remained friends. Like the old cliché: They were closer now than when they'd been living together.

Lots of old clichés seemed to be hitting home lately. Especially the one about no man on his deathbed ever wishing he'd spent more time at the office.

Will wished he'd spent more time with his daughter Kelly. She was a second-year medical student now at NYU and Will realized that he hardly knew her. Since he'd learned about the tumor, he'd come to regret bitterly all the opportunities he'd missed to be with Kelly when she was growing up.

Remorse had become a cold anvil, chained to his neck, dragging behind him wherever he went.

If only he'd known then . . .

He realized he'd been saying *if only* an awful lot lately.

Annie was looking at him now with hurt in her brown eyes. "You weren't going to tell me, were you."

"Sure I was. Eventually."

"I can't believe you're acting this way. You—the doctor's doctor, Mr. Modern Medicine. It's just not like you to refuse treatment."

"Did Dave tell you what they'll have to do to 'cure' me?"

"He said surgery and radiation."

"Did he give you any details?"

"No."

"I didn't think so. All right, then, *I'll* tell you. First they heavily radiate my oral cavity and throat for weeks to shrink the tumor. But in the process it shrivels up my esophagus as well, and so for months to come I'll only be able to swallow watery fluids, and those with difficulty, which is just as well because the radiation will kill off my taste buds and dry up my salivary glands, and I won't be able to taste anything anyway."

He saw Annie swallow.

"Then comes the surgery: a radical neck dissection. And I do mean *radical.* I lose my larynx, a big chunk of my tongue, and most of my right lower jaw. And then it's back for more radiation. And maybe chemo."

Annie's hand crept to her mouth. "Oh, God."

"I'll wind up with three-quarters of a face; I'll speak by burping or buzzing through a voice box; I'll eat by choking fluids and gruel down a strictured esophagus past a mutilated tongue that can't taste."

Annie turned and stumbled toward the sparsely furnished living room. She dropped into a chair.

"I had no idea!"

Will hesitated a moment, then followed and stood over her. He laid a hand on her shoulder. He knew Annie, knew her empathy. She *felt* for other people, shared their pain if they were hurting. Empathy could be a curse; he could imagine what she was feeling for him now. But her genuine distress warmed him—at least she still cared about him. He was sorry he'd had to dump it on her like that, but he saw no reason to pretty it up.

She looked up at him. "But at least you'll be alive."

"You call that living, Annie? That's not life—that's existence. And an empty one to boot: I can't practice in that state. And since I won't want to inflict my appearance on anyone, I'll wind up sitting around here alone, listening to my scratchy old records and watching my westerns. How many times do you think I can listen to 'Eight Miles High' and watch *Ride the High Country* before I finally jam the muzzle of a pistol into what's left of my mouth and end it all!"

Annie was cringing in the chair, staring at him. Will realized his voice had risen almost to a shout.

He turned away. "Sorry."

He hadn't realized how angry he was. He was reacting like every other cancer patient he had known, thinking it wasn't fair. And it wasn't! It wasn't goddamn *fair!*

Calmer now, he sighed and said, "When I hear myself talk like that, I think it sounds like it's all about vanity. But it's not vanity, Annie. It's dignity. Through my entire career I struggled to pre-serve my patients' dignity. I fought for their self-determination. I want the same for myself. I don't believe in life at any cost—not for me, anyway. I want to choose the manner of my leaving, and do not care to be sliced and diced, fried, and poisoned as I head for the exit."

He sensed movement behind him, then felt Annie's arms go around him. God, that felt good.

She sobbed into his back. "Oh, Will, oh, Will! I'm so sorry. I wish there was something I could do."

Suddenly he wanted to cry too, to turn and cling to her and bawl like a baby, to release all the screaming fear and remorse dammed up inside him. Instead, he covered her hands where they clasped over his abdomen and forced a laugh.

"Yeah. Me too. Got any magic?"

The phone rang.

It was in easy reach so he lifted the receiver.

"Dr. Burleigh?" said a woman's voice.

He recognized the accent. The woman from the place in Katonah. What was her name?

"Speaking."

"This is Maya. Can you see me tomorrow morning?"

He hesitated, wanting to say thanks but no thanks, but a part of him, a part that desperately wanted to live and figured he couldn't possibly make matters worse, wouldn't allow it.

"Sure," he said. "Ten o'clock okay?"

"Yes. I will see you then."

He hung up, wondering why he was wasting what little time he had left on a nutcase like Maya.

That wasn't fair. Enigmatic, magnetic, and certainly misguided, but Will had sensed that she was quite sane. And ethical as well—she'd wanted him to see a surgeon immediately.

But that didn't answer the question of why he was consulting a psychic healer.

Perhaps because she was a mysterious stone he'd encountered on this final stretch of his road. And though he was perfectly sure he'd find nothing under it, he didn't want to leave it unturned.

"Who was that?" Annie said from behind.

He didn't turn to look at her. "No one. No one who's going to make any difference, that is."

Katonah, NY

Will noticed a CLOSED sign in the window, but Maya opened the door immediately when he knocked.

She was wearing tan slacks and a dark blue polo shirt that lay snug around her small, high breasts.

"Closed?" he said.

"I did not want anyone else disturbing us."

He wondered what sort of traffic she got in such an understated, fringe locale.

"What are we going to be doing?"

"I want to finish what I began the other day."

"The thing with the tines and—what were they called?"

"Chakras. Yes. I never got to the last two, and one of them is very important."

Something was different in the way she was looking at him. Will couldn't put his finger on it, but she seemed somehow . . . closer. Odd, but that was the only way he could express it.

"But—"

"Please. Just let me finish. Then we can talk."

Will repressed a sigh as he followed her back down to the basement. He'd wanted this to be quick and clean: Can you help me and what's the first step? But he supposed he had to let her run through her rituals.

As before, he removed his shoes and socks and lay prone on the sand. Maya took up the greenish tine again, the one she'd used over his throat before, and rotated it in circles over the crown of his head. Her expression was grim as she switched to a bluish tine, plucked it, and moved that over the bridge of his nose. She leaned back a moment, closing her eyes, then she plucked the tine again, this time actually pressing it against the bridge of his nose.

Finally she rose and moved away. "Very well. I am through."

Will sat up and stared at her. She looked troubled.

"Something else wrong?"

She was rearranging her tines. She shook her head without looking up. "Nothing I did not already suspect."

He moved to the chair and began slipping back into his socks and shoes.

"What's that supposed to mean?"

She pulled the other chair around, seated herself, and faced him. She fixed him with her jade eyes.

"Talk to me."

"About what?"

"About yourself."

"Not much to talk about. I lead a pretty dull life."

"I called Savanna and asked her about you."

"And?"

"She says you are a wonderful doctor."

"Always liked Savanna," he said dryly. "A very perceptive woman."

Maya's lips twisted into a brief, wry smile, accenting her dimples. "Why did you not tell me you were a doctor?"

"I didn't think it was relevant to the diagnosis."

"But it is relevant to the mindset you bring."

"Is that so important?"

"It is everything. But back to Savanna: She went on so much

about you that I asked if she could introduce me to a few of your other patients."

"Really." Will wasn't sure he liked the idea of this woman investigating him. If anything, he should be investigating her. "Why?"

"To see if you are a healer, or merely a doctor."

Healer . . . the word on the window.

"So what am I?"

"You are loved."

Loved? Will snorted to hide a rush of embarrassment. "I hardly think—"

"No, it is true. The patients I spoke to love you. They say you are kind and caring, and give them all the time they need. They say when they are with you they feel they are your only patient. More than one told me they had called you in the night and you sent them to the emergency room. They figured you were passing them off to the emergency room staff, but when they arrived, they found you there waiting for them. I have not heard of many doctors who do that."

"Just part of doing the job."

"Then why are not all doctors loved?"

"I don't know about other doctors. And to tell you the truth, I don't really care. Managing my own practice was about all I could handle. I created my own little microcosm where I practiced my own style of medicine. And that involved listening. Listen well, and many times a patient will tell you exactly what's wrong with them—lay the diagnosis right out in front of you. Other times that's all people need—time to vocalize and someone to listen. All too often I think the prescription they carry away is nothing more than a Dumbo feather."

"I am sorry? A dumb . . . ?"

"You know . . . Dumbo. The Disney elephant."

"Oh, yes. Yes, of course."

"Well, Dumbo could fly just fine on his own, but he didn't believe that. He thought he needed that crow feather to do it."

She clapped her hands and laughed, and he found the sound delightful.

"A Dumbo feather. Yes, that is so true. I will have to remember that. And the fact that you see it is wonderful. It means you do not view yourself as some sort of deity dispensing cures. You know that sometimes you are only a facilitator."

"Whoa," he said. "Let's not get carried away here. I assure you all those years of med school and residency are worth something."

But what are they worth now? he wondered. NYU pre-med, Harvard medical, three years as an internal medicine resident at Beth Israel, almost two decades of clinical practice—all that training and experience vanishing into smoke.

Will shook it off. "You've got to know how the body functions and how its processes break down, and how pharmaceuticals work to mend it. If you haven't mastered that, you're going to kill people."

"But you need more than competence to be loved."

"Please—"

"Does that make you uncomfortable . . . being loved by your patients?"

"Well, love is such a strong word. I don't love them. I mean, I *like* them, I care about them, I want to do right by them. But love them . . . ?"

"Do you love anyone?"

"I love my daughter Kelly."

"Anyone else?"

"Annie . . . my ex."

"You love her? Then why is she 'ex'?"

"She feels she's better off without me."

"She left you."

Will nodded. "Yeah."

"Did you abuse her?"

He hesitated, wondering where this woman thought she got the right to ask that, then shrugged it off.

"How could I? I was never around."

"And that was the problem?"

"I think it all boils down to that. Staying with me and leaving me . . . I don't think she saw much difference, except that leaving offered her a chance to find what she needed, while staying with me . . ."

"You wouldn't change to keep her?"

"'Couldn't' is more like it. After Kelly went off to college and it was just the two of us in that house, she started wanting more from me and I didn't have it. I was up to my lower lip in my practice and she was bouncing off the walls of an empty house. And many times, even when I was with her, I wasn't really *with* her . . . I was thinking about some patient slipping away in the hospital . . . some puzzling set of symptoms I'd seen in the office that day. I wasn't there for her. I was physically present but I wasn't . . . *there.* And she knew it. The long and the short is, I didn't deliver."

Why am I telling her this? he wondered. Then figured, what did it matter? He wasn't going to be around long enough for anything he said to anyone to matter.

"Did you try—?"

"We tried everything, trust me: we went round and round for years, counseling, the whole bit. Let's just say we wore it out."

"Do you miss her?"

"Like crazy."

"Does she know that?"

"If you mean have I told her, no. A little late for that anyway. She found a new guy, they're going to marry."

"And you approve?"

"Yeah. He's a nice guy. He'll be good for her."

"And you're happy for her."

"Annie is a good person. She deserves to be happy."

She gave him a long stare. "I think you are a good person too, Dr. Burleigh."

What's this all about? he wondered. All this stroking made him uncomfortable.

"I try. I'm okay, I guess."

"You *guess?*"

"I'm not one for much introspection. Haven't got time for it."

Still she stared at him. "What is that quote about the life which is unexamined . . . ?"

"Being not worth living? Who was that? Socrates?"

"Plato."

"Right. Well, I've got a message for Mr. Plato: Bull. Besides, in my business, I spend my time examining other people's lives, not the other way around."

"Do you blame your practice for the failure of your marriage?"

"Me . . . my practice . . . we were one and the same. Somehow my patients always drew me away."

Maya leaned forward, her face intent. "Perhaps you could not help it."

"That's a cop-out."

"No. Listen to me. Perhaps some stronger force inside was driving you. Perhaps because you are more than a doctor . . . you are a healer. When the Mother chooses her healers, they cannot resist."

Not "the Mother" again.

"Let's not romanticize this," Will said. "I'm a doctor. A guy with a trade. Someone who's learned about the body and knows a few tricks about how to fix it."

"Surely it is more than a trade."

"Okay, maybe it is. It's just that sometimes I find myself trying to compensate for those docs who seem to think the M.D. degree confers godhood."

"But the fact remains, you were so devoted to your practice that it cost you your marriage. How do you explain that?"

Will shrugged. He didn't want to get into this. He'd been through it all during marriage counseling. He hadn't had an answer then, and he didn't have one now.

"Did you always want to be a doctor?" she said.

"Always . . . much to my father's chagrin. He wanted his only son to be a lawyer, join his firm." Will shook his head at the memories of their battles. "Never gave up. Went to his grave still trying to convince me to go back to law school and become a medical-legal specialist. But let's get off me and—"

"But that is why we are here: you."

"We're here because of this thing in my throat. Let's get to the bottom line here: Can you do for me what you did for Savanna?"

"No." She shook her head and looked away. "I dearly wish I could but . . ."

Will was surprised by the jolt of alarm that flashed through him. She couldn't turn him away!

"But what?"

"Savanna was accepting. She let me reach her. You . . . you have placed many many walls between yourself and someone like me."

"How can you say that? We haven't even spent an hour together."

She was looking at him again. "I can tell . . . your sixth chakra is completely blocked."

"So?"

"It's also called the third eye. Yours is essentially blind. It would take me years to help you as I helped Savanna."

"I don't have years."

"I know."

They sat in silence, Will wondering why he felt crushed. He didn't believe in any of this hokum anyway.

"What is your full name?" she said. "What does the 'W. C.' stand for?"

Will took a breath. He'd always hated his name. "Wilbur Cecil Burleigh."

Maya threw back her head and made a sound that was half laugh, half groan of dismay. "I should have known!"

"What's wrong?"

"Your mother must have sensed how you would turn out. Mothers know."

"I don't get it. They're family names."

"I have studied names. Each has a meaning, and I believe they attach to people for a reason. 'Wilbur' means the shining man, or the resolute brilliant one. Burleigh means dweller behind the fortress walls. And Cecil . . ." she shook her head. "Cecil means blind."

Wearily, Will pushed himself up from the chair.

"Then I guess there's no point in—"

"But there might be a way," she said softly.

"I'm listening."

"You will think it radical."

"Can't be more radical than what the surgeons and radiologists have in mind. Try me."

"You will have to put yourself completely in my hands."

He paused, thinking: You're talking to a control freak, lady. Be careful what you ask.

"I don't know if I like the sound of that."

"I am not sure yet what it will entail, and I know it will sound like a huge step to you. But it will be no small step for me either. I will have to put my own life on hold while I concentrate on yours."

"Why would you do that?"

"Because . . . ," She bit her lower lip. "Because for the longest time I've had the feeling that I was sent—or 'drawn' or 'guided'—here, to this place, at this time, for a purpose. And you may be that purpose."

Cue *The Twilight Zone* music, he thought.

"Hear me out," she said, as if she sensed him withdrawing. "Savanna comes to me, I help her; she in turn goes to you, and sends you to me." Maya's green eyes sparkled with excitement. "Don't you see? A circle has been closed, and now another one opens: You are a healer—a wounded healer—and I believe I am here to help you go on healing. But because you are the shining blind man in the fortress, you must learn to see before you can be healed. And you will not be able to see until we break down the walls of your fortress and let in the light. We must strip away all the layers of insulation you have built up over the years."

"Insulation? Against what?"

"Against the greatest healing force in the universe."

"Which is . . . ?"

"You will know it when you allow it to find you."

Will sighed. "Okay. I'll bite: What do I have to do?"

Maya rose and began a slow circuit of the basement. "You must liquidate all your belongings and assets, pension plans, everything."

"Ah, I see. The old sell-all-that-you-own-and-give-it-to-the-poor-and-follow-me routine."

"Follow me, yes, but put aside enough money for travel, and give only half to charity. The other half you will put into an irrevocable trust that will go to your daughter or your ex-wife or any charity upon your death."

A psychic healer talking about irrevocable trusts—Will's bullshit alarm began to howl. And yet, he was baffled.

"But the whole idea of my following you would be to circumvent a certain minor complication called death."

"The liquidation unburdens you of your lifelong accumulation of material baggage. Those possessions form one of your many walls, but it is the flimsiest, the one most easily breached."

"Easy for you to say. What happens on the outside chance that I don't die? Do I get the remaining half back?"

"No. The whole idea is to cut yourself off permanently from those possessions. Thinking about how and when and if you will get them back will only distract you. You must banish them from your life with no hope of ever retrieving them. That way they cannot distract you."

"Then who—?"

"Two years from now, if you are still alive, the remainder will go to me."

The alarms ringing in Will's head rose in pitch and volume.

"Oh, I see," he said slowly. "That will bring a windfall your way. Aren't you afraid it will 'burden' you?"

"Not at all." She gave him a level stare. "Because I will not have it for long. I have uses for it. And if indeed you are alive two years from now, can you say that I will not have earned it?"

She had him there. But Will knew there was a catch; had to be. He simply couldn't see it at the moment. Just for the hell of it, though, he decided to play along.

"Okay, let's say I do all that. Then what?"

"Then you must meet me in Mesoamerica, where we will seek out your own personal cure."

"Mesoamerica?"

"Maya country."

The Mayas came from Mexico, didn't they? Hunting for his own "personal cure" . . . really, this was getting more ridiculous by the minute.

But then again, going away with this strange and beautiful woman . . .

"And how long will this little trip take?"

"Two weeks at most—I hope."

That did it. Will stuck out his hand. "Nice meeting you, Maya. Thanks for your time, but I've got to be moving."

She clasped his hand with both of hers and held on.

"No. Please, Dr. Burleigh. Do not go."

He saw genuine concern in her eyes. For what? The money . . . or him?

"How much do I owe you?"

"Nothing. Please, I want you to think about—"

"With all due respect, I quite literally do not have time for this. I thought I'd give you a try, figuring I could spare a few days and a few bucks on the very outside chance that there might be something to this. But liquidate all my assets? Travel to Mexico and spend weeks looking for my 'personal cure'? Sorry. I've lined up better ways to spend my last months."

"What could be better than healing yourself?"

"Traveling to France, catching the harvest in Bordeaux, visiting the chateaux."

He'd spotted a notice in *The Wine Spectator* a few weeks ago and on a whim had booked the trip. He'd always wanted to see France. Finally he was going to do it.

Will gently pulled his hand free. "I wish you luck. You seem like a decent person who sincerely wants to help, but this stuff isn't for me."

"It is not just me who wants you healed," she said, following him as he trotted up the steps to the first floor. "So does your Mother."

He didn't look back. "I told you: my mother's dead—heart attack six years ago."

"You know very well that I did not mean your human mother—I meant the All-Mother."

"Oh, *that* mother. How could I forget about *her?*"

She went to the desk in the front room and removed a business card from the drawer.

"Never forget the All-Mother," she said, pressing the card into his hand. "She will give you a sign. Watch for it. She will smile on you to let you know that she wants you to be saved. Call me when she does."

Let me out of here!

"I'll keep my eyes open. Meanwhile, I've got to run. Bye."

And then he was through the door and back on the steaming sidewalk. Back in the real world. Relief poured through him.

He headed directly for his Rover. As he slid behind the wheel he glanced up and saw Maya standing in her doorway, watching him with her jade stare. She was saying something. He couldn't hear her, but her lips seemed to form the words, "You'll be back."

4

Grézillac, France

Will sat alone in the dark on the wrought iron settee under the cherry tree at the base of one of Chateau de Mouchac's towers. He swirled his glass of La Louvière 1988. By the light of the rising moon, he stared into the maelstrom of red liquid and asked himself for maybe the hundredth time since sunset, *Why am I here?*

A tour of the Bordeaux wine country, eleven people wandering the vineyards, seeing the ways different wines are made, visiting the famous chateaux for tastings.

Eat, drink, and be merry, for tomorrow we may die—not an empty cliché for Will. He'd been eating way too much cheese and foie gras, and drinking extraordinary amounts of wine. But merry? Not a chance.

Why am I here?

For the beauty? Yes, that sounded like a good reason. A few days in rural France, watching the wondrous changes in the light from hour to hour, were all it took to understand why Impressionism had developed here. Hell, it would have been a miracle if it *hadn't.*

Rural France . . . Will now considered the phrase redundant. On the train ride from Charles de Gaulle to Libourne he'd been amazed by how much of France was farmland—mile after mile after mile of planted fields. A country of farms and villages with a few cities plopped down here and there like fried eggs on a griddle.

As he'd traveled farther and farther south, he'd wondered when he would see the first vines. Then he'd entered the wine region and was soon wondering where he wouldn't see a vine. Every square inch of land that was not given over to the absolute necessities of life—things like a house, garage, or driveway—was planted with vines.

Chateau de Mouchac sat on a small rise in Grézillac, a tiny village in the Entre Deux Mers region of Bordeaux. Entre Deux Mers—Between Two Seas. Not really. Between two rivers was more like it. But since the Garonne and the Dordogne were so tidal, with the Atlantic surging miles upriver at high tide, Entre Deux Mers was not a complete misnomer.

Someone had begun building Mouchac back in the twelfth century. All that remained now of the original walls were what appeared to be low stone fences. The four towers and the current U-shaped house had been added in the fourteenth century.

Will marveled that all this had been completed long before Christopher was a gleam in Mr. Columbus's eye.

Mouchac had its own label, and its vineyards rolled away on the surrounding hills. Will had stood at his bedroom window this morning shortly after dawn, staring in wonder as the liquid rays of the rising sun poured across the tops of the rows of merlot and sauvignon blanc, etching the fields with stripes of golden fire.

Harvest was in progress. The white sauvignon grapes had been hauled to the winery out back and pressed this afternoon. The juice had been vatted to await the start of fermentation, and the air out here was rich with the yeasty-sour tang of the *fromage*, the discarded skins and stems, sitting now in a pulpy pile outside the pressing room. Delirious swarms of gnat-sized fruit flies would feast until the leftovers were carted away tomorrow.

He'd drunk the sparkling pousse rapière aperitif and nibbled some foie gras, but a casual remark by one of the tour's oenophiles had killed his appetite. No longer able to sit still, he'd excused himself from the long, glass-laden oak table and wandered outside, taking a bottle of LaLouviere with him. He'd considered strolling the tree-lined path down to Grézillac's village center, but decided against it. Not much there beyond a few stone houses and mankind's three most durable and indispensable institutions: a church, a graveyard, and a bar. Instead, he'd watched the setting sun ignite pink clouds in the azure sky.

The remark . . . he'd heard it a dozen times in the past few days, but it had struck home with vicious force tonight. They were tasting a new red, straight from the barrel, and one of the men had said, "Very nice—this should open up beautifully in another five to seven years."

Five to seven years? Will had thought. I don't have five to seven *months!*

Now the nearly full moon had risen and he was still on the iron bench, suffering the perseverative question: *Why am I here?*

Damn. I can't say I'm making new friends . . . I'll never see these people again. I can't even say I'm storing up memories . . . I won't be around to remember any of this.

And so he was in a rather black mood when Catherine found him.

"Room for another on that seat?" she said.

Will shifted to his right and lifted the bottle out of her way.

Catherine was average height, fortyish, and a bit on the plump side, but lively and pretty in a Lynn Redgrave sort of way. The tour consisted of four couples, plus Catherine and her brother, with Will as odd man out. The tour director had seated them together at the first dinner, and they tended to pair off on the daily vineyard walks. During those walks he'd learned that she too was divorced but had nothing good to say about her ex other than the fact that he was wealthy enough to afford whopping alimony payments.

Will had gathered from a few chance remarks by some of the other males on the tour that they had a pool going as to when he and Catherine would wind up in the sack.

Sorry, boys, he thought. No winner.

He and Annie had had a passably active if not terribly inventive sex life during their marriage, and Will had had a few brief flings since the divorce, but nothing serious. His sex drive, however, seemed to have shifted into low gear since he'd read the path report on the tumor. In fact, sex rarely crossed his mind these days.

Even if that weren't the case, Catherine could be a little wearing. She seemed to think she was an authority on everything and had a tendency to expound on any subject, no matter how common or widely known.

And to further dampen any nascent lust, damned if he hadn't begun recently to sense a swelling at the back of his tongue. His imagination? Or was the primary tumor finally announcing its presence?

If his thoughts were on any woman, it was Maya. Why, he couldn't say. He almost wished she were here. She was a kook, certainly, but an intriguing one, and more interesting than anyone on this tour.

"Are you all right?" Catherine said.

"Oh, I'm just great," he told her.

"Good. Because you didn't look so hot when you walked out. We all thought you might be sick."

"Just needed some air."

"I know what you mean," she said, moving closer. "I—"

He felt her stiffen and glanced at her. Catherine was leaning forward, staring at the sky.

"Oh, my God, will you look at that!"

Will looked up and was startled to see a piece missing from an upper corner of the moon, as if some celestial predator had taken a bite out of it. Just moments ago it had been almost perfectly round.

Catherine bounded from the seat and dashed toward the chateau, calling for everyone to come out.

Will stayed where he was while the rest of the party emerged from the dining hall and gathered in Mouchac's courtyard, oohing and ahhing as they gazed skyward. Catherine returned to his side, but remained standing and staring at the shrinking moon.

"This morning's paper had mentioned that an eclipse was due," she said, "but I'd forgotten all about it. It isn't going to be a full eclipse, though."

The upper three quarters of the moon were gone now, leaving only a glowing horizontal crescent hanging in the sky.

"Looks like a big grin, doesn't it," Catherine said. "Like the

Cheshire Cat in *Alice.*" She slipped into her lecture mode. "The monthly crescents of the moon are a result of the angle of the sun, you know. This is different. That's the earth's shadow up there. So in a sense, the earth is making the cat disappear, leaving us with just the smile."

Will's glass slipped from his fingers, spilling wine on the grass as he shot to his feet.

"What? What did you say?"

"That it's good old Mother Earth creating that smile up there."

Shaken, he took a step toward her. "Who are you? Who told you to say that?"

Catherine backed away. He could see the alarm on her face. "What are you talking about, Will?"

His head was buzzing like a wasp nest. "Who sent you?"

She moved further away. "I think you've had too much to drink."

She turned and hurried toward the others in the courtyard, leaving him alone in the dark under the tree. Will looked up at the glowing crescent grinning down at him, and remembered Maya's parting words.

. . . *the All-Mother . . . will give you a sign. Watch for it. She will smile on you to let you know that she wants you to be saved.*

This was crazy. Had she known he was coming to France? Had she known there'd be a partial eclipse? Possible, sure, but . . . damn!

"Too much to drink?" he muttered, locating his empty glass and picking up the bottle of Graves. "Oh, no. I haven't had anywhere *near* enough to drink."

With a trembling hand he poured himself half a glass and wandered farther away from Mouchac. He stopped at the edge of the vineyard and leaned on one of the vine row end posts, careful to avoid the thorns of the traditional rose bush planted there.

Calm down, he told himself. This eclipse didn't just happen out of the blue—it was expected, scheduled. Catherine had read about it in the paper. This was a regular phenomenon. Nothing supernatural about it. Certainly no All-Mother smiling down at him.

And yet, it looked *exactly* like a smile. He realized that if he were back in the States now instead of here, he wouldn't have seen a damn thing—it was mid-afternoon on the East Coast.

But I *am* here, he thought. And I've been asking myself why.

Against his will, his thoughts gravitated to Maya and her proposal.

Will already had an irrevocable trust set up for Kelly, so she was taken care of. Annie would have no financial problems after she remarried. So he could see no reason why he couldn't liquidate his assets, give half away to, say, cancer research, and stick the rest in a trust set up as Maya had described.

He had no illusions: Before year's end, Kelly would wind up with the contents of that trust as well.

And then what? Head off with Maya into the wilds of Latin America—what she'd called "Mesoamerica"—and search for a cure?

Yeah, right.

Then again, hadn't he wanted to spend what little time he had left traveling? Why not do the traveling in "Mesoamerica"?

Will poured some more wine.

Yes, really . . . why not? Why the hell not?

Not in search of a cure, but just for the sheer damn bloody hell of it. A truly crazy, futile, wrongheaded gesture, but in some perverse way its very craziness, futility, and wrongheadedness appealed to him.

In his entire life, when had he ever done *anything* on impulse? Never. If he was ever going to act on a reckless urge, this was the time. Because soon he'd be unable to act, and not too long after that, he'd have no more impulses, reckless or otherwise.

Yes, Will Burleigh, he thought. Why not choose something utterly foolish as the last grand gesture of your otherwise safe, sane, staid, straight-laced, predictable life? Go off with a New Age healer, go through all the motions, perform every ritual she prescribes, all without one shred of hope of a cure.

But who knows? he thought. Maybe I'll be surprised.

He'd lived his whole life believing that the universe functioned according to the physical laws of matter and energy set down by human science. He'd always believed those laws to be right.

But now he realized that a small desperate part of him ached for them to be wrong.

He lifted his glass and toasted the grin in the sky, growing lopsided now as earth's shadow moved on.

"Mesoamerica, here I come!"

5
Westchester County, NY

What had seemed like such an easy, straightforward decision in France turned out to be a complicated process back home.

Will had broken off from the tour and returned to the U.S. the day after the eclipse, but he didn't contact Maya immediately. Before he became involved with this woman, he wanted to know more about her. So he got in touch with Max Eppinger, his long-time lawyer and an old friend. Max put him on to a private investigator named Vincent Terziski.

Will met with Terziski, a heavyset man with a florid complexion, and hired him to check out the mysterious woman "healer" with the shop in Katonah.

The detective stopped by Will's apartment two days later. He was sweating, wheezing, and smelled like an ashtray. Will wondered about the man's blood pressure and the state of his coronary arteries, but said nothing. He'd learned the hard way that some people don't appreciate unsolicited medical advice.

He listened to Terziski's initial report.

"Don't have much," he said, "and most of what I've got is from secondary sources."

"Meaning?"

"From applications to open her business, stuff like that. I mean, I know where she *says* she got a degree, but I haven't checked with the school itself yet. Anyway, your gal's full name's Maya Quennell, which made my job a helluva lot easier since there aren't a whole lot of people with either name. She was born thirty-four years ago in Oran, Algeria, of a French father and a Mayan mother. Grew up in Paris, attended the Sorbonne—don't know if she ever graduated—and supposedly has a philosophy degree from Berkeley."

Berkeley, Will thought. Why am I not surprised?

"She's got a checking account with roughly eighteen thousand on deposit, but no other tangible assets, not even a car. She lives in the apartment above her storefront. No arrest record for fraud or anything else; and not a single consumer complaint against her."

So far, so good, Will thought.

"That's all?"

"So far, yeah. I did find a Maya Quennell who was arrested during a logging site protest back in 1972, but that can't be the same girl—she's not old enough. Like I said before, I'll be checking out the schools and such for confirmation, but all in all I'd say your gal looks pretty clean right now. Wouldn't mind having a set of her fingerprints, though. Any chance—?"

"I don't think so," Will said quickly.

Scenes from old movies about pocketing a cocktail glass to secure a set of prints flashed behind his eyes.

"She didn't happen to give you a crystal or anything like that, did she?"

And then Will remembered: "She did give me a business card."

He went to his bedroom and found it on the dresser. He picked it up by the corner and brought it to the detective.

"That might do it," Terziski said, inspecting the glossy surface as he held it by the edges. "Now give me something with a set of your prints on it so I'll know which is which."

Although he told Terziski to go ahead with the next phase, Will was fairly satisfied that Maya wasn't a bunco artist. He stopped by her storefront that afternoon.

"Dr. Burleigh," she said, her tone cautious, her expression hopeful. "You are back so soon from your trip?"

"France wasn't what I needed," he said, and left it at that. No way was he going to tell her about the eclipse. "I decided I wanted something a little more exotic. Like Mexico, maybe?"

"This is true?" she said, her eyes widening. Was that elation in her voice? "This is what you wish?"

"I think so . . . if your offer is still open."

"Yes, it is. Yes, it most certainly is. What happened? How did the Mother change your mind?"

"This has nothing to do with your All-Mother. This is my own decision."

"Yes," she said. "Yes, of course."

But Will didn't think she believed him.

"How soon can we leave?" he said.

"As soon as I make arrangements for other people I am caring for, and you liquidate your assets, as we discussed."

"You still think that's necessary?"

"Absolutely."

Will began liquidating. He'd already sold his practice; he sold off his collection of old sixties rock to a collector's store in Manhattan called Fynyl Vynyl, and donated all his western videotapes to the Mt. Kisco branch of the public library.

As for his rented townhouse, the complex had a waiting list of prospective tenants and Will had no problem finding someone to take over the balance of his lease.

The rest wasn't so easy, mainly because Max Eppinger became convinced that Will had lost his mind. Max was almost seventy now and refused to retire; his body was wizened, his back stooped, but his mind remained as sharp as ever. Max had handled all Will's legal affairs since he arrived in Westchester—everything from house closings to incorporating his medical practice.

Max ranted about how much money Will would lose in penalties and taxes by prematurely emptying his pension funds, but when he learned the details of the trust, about how the contents would go to a stranger if Will were alive two years from now, he urged Will to have himself committed.

At times Will wondered if that truly might not be a bad idea. Usually those wonderings occurred when he was lying awake in the bed of the townhouse he'd be vacating in a week. When he considered that he'd soon be homeless and penniless, that he'd be leaving his country and traveling with a strange woman into the heart of a land where he knew only a smattering of the language, a worm of doubt and unease would begin wriggling through his gut. Maybe Max was right. Maybe the stress of having a terminal illness had unhinged him.

But Will managed to struggle through those moments. He'd made up his mind about this and he was going through with it: Will Burleigh was going to have a goddamn adventure before he died.

He went so far as to buy a laptop computer to keep a record of the trip. He backfilled to his first meeting with Maya, then vowed to keep a daily record.

Maybe if he didn't get back, his story would.

Finally, it was done: he had a few thousand in the bank for travel expenses, and the rest—half had gone to cancer research, and half lay in a trust that would go to Kelly upon his death, or to Maya Quennell if he was still alive two years from now. Only Max knew about the trusts.

As for the trip, he told Annie simply that he was going to Mexico, never hinting as to why, or with whom.

Then came the really hard part: telling Kelly.

"What's the matter with your voice, Daddy?" she said. They were lunching at Coming or Going, a little country French place in midtown. Kelly looked so much like her mother Will could almost believe he was sitting with Annie half a lifetime ago. "You sound hoarse."

He did sound hoarse. Could it be . . . ?

No, the tumor couldn't have progressed that far already.

"Just a little cold," he said, not wanting to worry her. "And maybe a lot of regret."

"For what?"

"For not being a better father."

He'd promised himself on the way in to the city that he wasn't going to get maudlin, but here he was, feeling bad about all those missed opportunities.

"Now please don't start that again," Kelly said, reaching across the table and taking his hand. "You're much too hard on yourself. Even when you weren't around in person, you were there in spirit. And it's not as if you were with another woman, or hanging out at a bar shooting pool and getting loaded. I always knew where you were, always knew you were doing good. You inspired me, Dad. If you hadn't, would I be in med school now? But the most important thing you gave to me is honesty. You never lied, never were a hypocrite. You always lived your values, Dad. That's incredibly precious; it's an example I'll try to live up to my entire life."

Will felt a pressure in his chest, an unbearable tightness in his throat. He blinked back tears as he held up his hand.

"Stop," he whispered. "You'll have me bawling like a newborn in a second."

"Well, it's true. You have nothing to ask forgiveness for . . . except for not treating that tumor."

He saw that Kelly was puddling up now. Will squeezed her hand. "Kelly, honey, we've been over—"

"I know, I know," she said quickly, wiping her eyes with her napkin, "but I can't help feeling that you're leaving me instead of being taken away. It's . . . it's almost . . . selfish."

Is it? Will wondered. Am I being selfish?

But it was his life, wasn't it? If he couldn't decide how his own life would end, what did he have? Was there a more fundamental human right?

He promised Kelly he'd keep in touch from Mexico by phone or e-mail, and he left wondering if he'd ever see his daughter again.

The hoarseness worried him. He thought he felt a fullness in the back of his throat when he swallowed. And when he checked his neck that night he discovered another enlarging node on the left side.

The next day he paid a visit to Dave who blanched when he reexamined Will's throat. He scheduled another MRI that afternoon and they reviewed the results immediately after.

"Shit!" Dave said. "I told you it was aggressive, Will, but it's beyond that—it's spreading like wildfire. My God, if you don't want the surgery, at least throw some rads into that thing to slow it down."

Will fought a surge of nausea as he stared at the images. He was no radiologist, but even he could see the rampant progress of the tumor . . . the "traitorous tissue," as Maya had called it.

"Captain Carcinoma," Will said as the name struck him.

Dave looked at him. "What?"

"The tumor . . . that's its name. It's leading a mutiny and trying to take over the ship."

"What the hell are you talking about?"

"Nothing. Forget it. Look—not a word of this to Annie, right? At least not until I come back from Mexico."

"Mexico?" Dave's expression was a mixture of anger and incredulity. "You're not seriously thinking of traveling?" He pointed at the films. "You could be heading for a carotid blowout!"

Carotid blowout . . . Will hadn't considered that. The tumor could erode through the wall of one of the frankfurter-caliber arteries running up each side of his throat. If that happened, the resulting massive hemorrhage would drain away his life in minutes.

He could think of worse ways to go.

"Just for a couple of weeks."

"Christ, Will! If you don't have a blowout, in a couple of weeks you'll be on IV's because you won't be able to swallow!"

That hit hard. Will leaned back and closed his eyes.

A couple of weeks?

Maya was getting ready to leave ahead of him—"To prepare the way," she'd said. He was to link up with her in Mexico a few days later. But how could he risk leaving the country if . . . ?

This changed nothing, damn it. The tumor had taken charge of the rest of his life, but it wasn't taking charge of this.

And if he was going to die, maybe Maya's Mesoamerica was the place to do it. No one to watch him suffer, no one to take over and stick him on life support if he became too weak to protest.

Yes, now more than ever he wanted to leave on his adventure.

But he had to ask Dave a big favor first. . . .

Mesoamerica

Where are we?

Will stared out the window of the battered Cessna two-seater at the lush beer-bottle green terrain sliding by below. He felt as if he'd been flying over Mexico for days. The trip had started early in the morning at JFK. A few hours ago his DC-10 had dropped through the ochre haze that passed for air in Mexico City. He'd gone through customs and hopped a jet to Villahermosa Aeropuerto where this single-prop rattletrap had been waiting for him. So now, after his third takeoff of the day, he was in the air again.

Conversation was hopeless. Even if he could make himself heard over the deafening roar and bone-rattling vibrations of the plane, his rudimentary Spanish wouldn't get him too far with Diego, the pilot.

That he'd learned at the airport when he tried to pry some information out of the young Mexican. Will was able to establish that Diego was indeed the pilot Maya had hired for him, but as for where

Diego was taking him, the best Will could learn was, "South . . . we go south."

So Will spent the flight gazing out the window.

Like France, where he'd expected the whole country to look like Paris, Mexico surprised him. He'd assumed he would see the desert settings of *The Magnificent Seven* or *The Wild Bunch*. Instead, it looked more like Ireland. All he'd seen since arriving were endless stretches of green mountains. Now the mountains were giving way to jungles, but the pervasive green rolled on below as they headed farther and farther south.

South. Villahermosa was in Tabasco, already pretty far into the tail end of the country. Not much more of Mexico south of there. After that, they'd be in Belize or Guatemala. Will didn't know much about Guatemala, but didn't like what he did know: guerrillas, military patrols, checkpoints, death squads, the whole banana republic thing. He wanted no part of that.

The worm of unease, the worm with whom Will had formed a close personal relationship during the past few weeks, began its familiar wriggle through his gut.

Things had moved so quickly after his meeting with Dave. When he'd called Maya to tell her he had to leave right away or not at all, she'd sounded almost panicked. Timing was everything, she'd said. She would have to leave immediately. She'd called his travel agent and detailed the arrangements to make for him, and told him she'd link up with him down here . . . in Mesoamerica.

A tap on his shoulder drew Will from his reverie. Diego was saying something unintelligible over the noise and pointing to a long valley dead ahead. Will saw an oblong clearing in the jungle.

What? Was he saying they were going to land? *There?* God, it wasn't a landing strip—it was barely even a field. He couldn't be serious.

When the Cessna banked into a descending turn, Will decided Diego was indeed serious. He looked around—anywhere but below. Off to the west he spotted a low bank of storm clouds, chugging along just above the jungle like a great gray frigate plowing through a sea of green, but it seemed to be moving away.

Nowhere did he see a sign of civilization. Wasn't there a town nearby? Or even a village?

Diego dropped his plane into a long, low glide, just inches from the tree tops, and brought the Cessna in for a brain-jarringly bumpy landing on the rutted, puddled soup of red mud and grass. When they finally slalomed to a stop less than fifty feet from the trees, Diego idled the engine and slapped Will on the thigh.

"Estamos aquí," he said, grinning.

Will looked around. "Where the hell is 'here'?"

"Aquí. Aquí-aquí-aquí."

The jungle pushed against the periphery of the clearing, its clustered trees jostling each other as they edged inward like a crowd around an accident.

"I don't think this is a 'here' where I want to be," Will said.

Suddenly he wanted *out* of 'here,' to be back in the good old U.S. of A. He didn't care if he'd have to move into a homeless shelter, it was better than being left alone in this foreign and overwhelmingly green wasteland. Panic began to sink its claws into him, tearing at the inner walls of his chest. How had he ever let himself get into this mess? What had he been thinking? Or had he been thinking at all?

No way he was getting out of this plane. He was about to tell Diego to turn it around and buzz him out of here when an open, beat-up, mud-splattered two-seater Jeep bounded into the clearing. It slewed to a halt and a spindly-armed, barrel-chested little man jumped out. He was dressed in some sort of tunic made of coarse white cotton. Will's attention homed in on the machete thrust through the embroidered belt around his waist. He trotted barefooted to Will's door and pulled it open.

"Señor Burleigh?" he said with a smile.

He had a round head covered with lank black hair, and bright dark eyes set in a face the color and texture of a baked apple. His smile revealed big white teeth outlined with gold; the metal gleamed in the sunlight, framing his top incisors like Old Master paintings.

Will hesitated, tempted to say that Señor Burleigh wouldn't be coming, but Diego knew the truth.

"That's me."

"Bueno! Maya, she send me." He thrust out a thickly callused hand. "I am Ambrosio."

Will shook hands. "Where's Maya?"

"We go to meet her now. She arrive two days ago. She wait for us in the hills."

"What hills?"

"Not far. You will see."

Another moment of indecision: Will felt he needed to see a familiar face in this alien place.

"Come," Ambrosio said. "We must go. Where is your bag?"

Will didn't budge. "How do you know Maya?"

"She is Ambrosio's kinswoman," the little man said.

Time to make a decision: stay or go. What would the Duke do in this situation?

Pushing aside his growing anxiety about all the uncertainties he was facing if he stepped out of this plane, Will sucked in a breath and decided to plunge ahead. He wrestled his large duffel bag from behind the seats and jumped to the ground.

Uncertainty was what an adventure was all about; remove the unpredictables and it became a guided tour.

And yet . . .

As he watched Diego wheel his Cessna about and gun it back down the clearing, Will could not escape the terrifying feeling that he was being marooned in the jungle. He waved, but Diego didn't wave back.

Ambrosio took the duffel bag and swung it onto his back. "We go now. Yes?"

"Yes."

At least he had a man Friday of sorts with him.

As he started walking he looked around at the green wilderness and thought, I'm either a very brave man, or a very foolish one. But either way, I'm a man who hasn't much to lose.

Had that been Maya's purpose in "unburdening" him of his assets? To make him reckless?

It seemed to be working.

He realized he was bathed in sweat. Some of it nervous sweat, no doubt, but the rest because it was *hot*. And wet. He'd thought the heat had been stifling back in New York, but that had been nothing compared to this. He bet he could grab a handful of air and wring a shot glass of water out of it.

Maya had warned him to dress light and in white. Will was glad he'd listened. Glad too that he'd bought waterproof hiking boots for the trip as he sloshed behind Ambrosio toward the Jeep. Small samples of the vehicle's original dark green finish, and swatches of its canvas top were visible through the thick coat of red mud that encased it. The twin arcs of clean glass on the windshield looked like watchful eyes.

"We have many, many rains," Ambrosio said. His English was good, and Will was glad for that.

"Does it ever stop?"

Ambrosio sniffed the air. "Chac sends us two more storms, Ambrosio thinks, and then he leave us alone."

"Chac?"

"The god of rain and storms."

Will winced as Ambrosio tossed the duffel into the Jeep's rear compartment. "I have a computer in there."

"A computer?" he said, flashing his gold-lined teeth. "We have no electricity here, señor."

"I have batteries," Will said. He'd brought extra lithium ion packs. "And I can always plug into your cigarette lighter."

Ambrosio shrugged and climbed in behind the wheel. "You will not need a computer where we are going."

Will figured he'd be the judge of that, but didn't challenge the little man.

"Is Maya far?" he said.

"She is miles away, on the other side of the valley. This is the closest a plane can land."

"And just where is this?"

"In the jungle."

"I know that. But what country?"

"Maya country. This is where Ambrosio was born."

Maya country . . . did that mean Maya the woman, or Maya the people? Will assumed he meant the people.

"But Maya country could mean Mexico, Belize, or Guatemala."

"Si." He started the engine. "You are thirsty?"

Will couldn't tell if Ambrosio was being evasive or merely obtuse. But he was thirsty. The bottle of Poland Spring he'd bought at JFK had run out long ago.

He nodded. "I could use a drink."

"Bueno."

Ambrosio worked the shift and the Jeep leaped backward—directly into the long ungainly trunk of a palm tree. Will cried out in alarm as something heavy landed on the canvas top and bounced off.

Next thing he knew, Ambrosio was hopping out of the Jeep and pulling his machete from his belt. He picked up a pale green coconut from the ground, hefted it in his hand, did *whack-whack-whack!* with the blade against its top, and then he was handing it through the doorway.

Will peered through the two-inch opening and found the cavity half filled with thin white liquid. Coconut milk. He sipped. It wasn't cold, but it was cool, mildly coconut-flavored, and definitely refreshing. Ambrosio had opened one for himself and was quaffing the contents, letting it dribble over his chin. He tossed his away and looked at Will.

"Another?"

Will hadn't finished his yet. "No mas, gracias."

Ambrosio grinned. "Muy bueno! Habla Espanol?"

"Not as well as you speak English, I'm afraid."

Ambrosio resumed his place behind the steering wheel, and this time they moved forward. He wheeled toward an opening in the greenery and headed along a rutted path. Will could make out only one set of tire tracks in the mud, the ones Ambrosio had made on his way here.

And then they were among the trees, so thick and huge, so intensely green and *old*, Will felt as if he'd somehow slipped back into the Cretaceous and that dinosaurs were lurking just ahead. The jungle quickly closed around them, over them, behind them, and the clearing slipped from view.

He fought a wave of claustrophobic angst, but it eased as Ambrosio began pointing out the local flora and fauna: squat palmettos, fluorescent parrots and macaws, the huge leaves of elephant taro, orange-beaked toucans, ocote pitch pines, a scurrying, brown, tailless paca, graceful acacias, chattering spider monkeys, and a spotted boa constrictor hanging from a eucalyptus branch.

Nothing here seemed to live alone. The trees were draped with lianas, with some of the vine trunks as thick around as a man's thigh. These in turn were layered with gray-green epiphytic growths and the occasional bright splotch of an orchid.

The sheer density of life here awed Will. He felt as if he were bumping along a capillary in some huge living organism.

"See those trees there?" Ambrosio said, pointing to a cluster of trunks with dark fluted bark and high leaves. "That is mahogany. Many *dzul* come here to cut it down and take it way."

"Dzul?"

"Foreigners. They come and cut-cut-cut, and never make peace with Yumtzil." He glanced at Will as if anticipating the question. "Yumtzil is the forest lord. Bad thing to forget forest lord."

"I'll remember that. Are Chac and Yumtzil Maya gods?"

"Si. We have many, many gods."

"Does Maya—not the people, your kinswoman—worship those gods?"

Ambrosio shook his head. "Maya is half dzul. She has her own ways, and they are much older than ours."

Older? Will was hardly an authority, but he didn't think American civilization got much older than the Mayas'.

And he thought he'd detected something new in Ambrosio's voice as he spoke of his kinswoman, but couldn't quite identify it.

"Does she offend your gods with her different ways?"

Ambrosio laughed. "No. Our gods are not jealous like yours."

"Like mine?" Will hadn't had been much of a churchgoer since he was a teenager, but he was still nominally a Presbyterian.

"Dzul gods—very jealous."

"Oh, I see. The Christian God."

"And Jewish God and Moslem God. All want to be the only god. Maya gods not like that. All live together. Much better that way."

"Can't argue with that. So what do your people think of Maya and her 'old ways'?"

"She is sometimes called *curandera*, a healer, and some call her *Ixchel*—'She-of-the-Rainbow.'"

"A lovely name," Will said. Had her jade eyes earned her that one?

"And some even call her *Xtabay*."

Will saw Ambrosio bite his lip as if he'd said something he shouldn't have.

"What does Xtabay mean?"

Ambrosio sighed. "Xtabay is a spirit who lures men deep into the woods and abandons them there."

Will felt his insides constrict into a fearful knot. Is that what Maya's got planned for me?

"But do not believe that," Ambrosio added quickly. "That is just an old tale used to frighten young men. The people who call her that do so because they do not understand her ways. Others, usually ones who follow the dzul god, call her *bruja*."

Will knew that word: *witch*.

"What do you call her?"

"Ambrosio calls her *sabia* . . . the wise one."

And now Will identified the mystery note in Ambrosio's tone: reverence.

"Mira!" Ambrosio said suddenly, pointing.

Something brightly colored and feathered darted across the path in front of them.

"A peacock!" Will said.

"No-no, señor. That is a turkey."

A turkey in the jungle. Imagine that. "Too bad you don't have Thanksgiving down here," Will said.

"Like in the U.S.?" Ambrosio shook his head. "No, señor. We do not give thanks that the dzul came to our land."

The sides of the path rose gradually until they were traveling in a gully, with the jungle floor slipping by at eye level. They came to a huge puddle, but Ambrosio never slowed. He plowed straight ahead as muddy water the color of old blood flew in gouts to either side, bathed the windshield, and sprayed through the doorways.

And as the Jeep rolled onto the opposite shore, the engine sputtered and died.

Ambrosio cursed in a number of languages as he turned the ignition key. The starter whined but the motor didn't turn.

"Maybe the wires are wet," Will said, shaking the mud off his right arm. He wasn't sure what that meant, but he'd heard it before and it sounded reasonable. "Give them a moment and they should dry."

Ambrosio muttered something about "waterproof" and popped the hood release. Will joined him at the front of the Jeep and helped him lift the hood.

Ambrosio groaned at the sight of the engine splattered with mud.

Will knew next to nothing about cars. He could look inside someone's abdomen and identify every organ and blood vessel and describe their functions in minute detail; put him in front of a car engine, however, and he was a stuttering bumpkin.

But you didn't need to be a *Popular Mechanics* subscriber to know that mud and the internal combustion engine did not mix. This one looked as if it had hemorrhaged.

Ambrosio worked on it for half an hour, wiping it clean, drying the wires, checking the connections . . . but the engine refused to turn over.

Finally he leaned back and stared upward. What was he looking at? He couldn't see the sky through the green canopy overhead.

He turned to Will. "Ambrosio must go get help."

"How far is that?"

"Miles."

Will looked down the gully. It looked walkable. "All right. Let's go."

"No. Not that way. Too many miles that way. Too far." He pointed into the thick of the jungle. "Ambrosio will go that way."

"And leave me here?"

No way, José.

"It is better." He pulled out his machete and made chopping motions at the jungle. "Ambrosio can go fast this way, but not with you. Dark will come." He pointed to the Jeep. "You stay. You can put up the sides and close the back. You will be safe until Ambrosio returns."

He turned and struck off into the brush.

"Wait!" Will shouted, fighting panic.

"Do not be afraid," the little man called back. "Ambrosio will come back soon!"

And then he was gone. Will could hear him crashing through the brush, but the vegetation had closed around him. Soon even his sounds were swallowed up by the green wall.

Will took two steps toward where he'd last seen him, then stopped. Ambrosio wasn't taking a shortcut, he was *making* one.

He's right, Will told himself. I'll only slow him up if I tag along.

And the idea of stumbling through this jungle in the dark, even with Ambrosio . . .

Yet Will couldn't help but remember Ambrosio's remark about Xtabay . . . the spirit who lures men deep into the woods and abandons them there.

Well, I'm plenty deep in the woods, he thought. And now I've been abandoned.

Don't get dramatic.

Ambrosio will come back soon. . . .

Will believed that. He didn't have unerring judgment about people, but Maya and Ambrosio seemed like good people.

I'll be all right, he told himself. This is just a bump in the road. Things will turn out fine. Don't let this get in the way of the adventure.

Movement on the ground caught his eye. Pieces of green leaf were walking across the gully. He bent for a closer look. No, the leaf bits weren't walking, they were being carried. By ants. A whole line of them . . .

Will squatted and saw another line of ants heading the other way, hundreds, thousands of little leafcutters traveling an invisible two-lane highway that crossed the floor of the gully. The burdened ants headed west, the empty-handed ones traveled east for another load.

Rising, he closed his eyes and sniffed the air. He found it ripe with the effluvia of life and death, the perfume of flowers, the musk of decay.

He listened. Since his arrival his ears had been jammed with man-made noise—the roar of the Cessna's motor, the purr of the Jeep's engine, Ambrosio's chatter. Now they were silent and the sounds of the jungle filled the air around him. The splats of leftover rainwater dropping lazily from leaf to leaf on its way to the ground, the high sharp calls of birds, the staccato chitter of monkeys, the cheeps of tree frogs, all set against the high-tension buzz of flies and cicadas.

Rain forest Muzak.

The quotidian rhythm of jungle life continued uninterrupted, taking no notice of him.

Will slapped at a stinging spot on his neck, and his hand came away with a dead mosquito on his palm. Well, something was taking notice of him. Maybe it would be a good idea to close up the Jeep now.

He stepped around to the rear and found the door flaps under his duffel. He also found an extra machete. He pulled it out and hefted it. The handle was cheap plastic, the long flat blade a dull black except for the steely glint along its honed edge, but somehow he felt better knowing he had it. He gave it a few practice swings, then slipped it through his belt.

The door flaps snapped into place easily, and he zipped the rear panel closed. There. That should keep out the bugs very nicely.

Just for the hell of it, he slipped behind the wheel and tried the ignition. No luck. The damn engine still refused to turn over.

The enclosed Jeep was hot and stuffy now, so he stepped out again. He considered pulling out his laptop and putting down the events of the day, but he was thirsty. He had a machete; all he had to do was find a coconut and chop it open as Ambrosio had.

He strolled up the gully, looking for a coconut palm. After a few dozen paces, the sound of running water caught his ear. It seemed to be coming from somewhere ahead and to the right.

A stream or a river maybe. Even better than a coconut.

As he moved on, looking for a break in the brush, he thought he saw a patch of sunlight beyond the roadside trees. That could only mean some sort of clearing. He found a narrow path into the undergrowth, probably an animal trail, climbed up the bank, and followed it in.

The going was slightly uphill and fairly easy for a couple of hundred feet. Along the way he noticed a dark brown, two-foot mound to his right. The ants moving in and out of the hole atop their hill were a good ten times larger than the leafcutters he'd seen before. He shuddered at a brief nightmare image of tripping and falling into *that*, and moved on.

Another twenty feet or so and he came to a thick tangle of bush and vine. Whatever had made the trail apparently squeezed under the tangle. Will wasn't about to try that, but he sensed that the clearing was just beyond.

He pulled out his machete and began hacking. It wasn't easy work, and his shirt was soaked with sweat by the time he broke through. He grinned. He'd made it to the clearing. But what he saw straight ahead brought him up short.

A pyramid.

It sat in the center of the clearing, basking in a pool of sunlight angling in over the treetops. Will had read up on the Maya in the past week, and had seen pictures of the temples and pyramids at Tulum and Chichen Itza. This one resembled those, but not as large; and in much worse condition. The jungle had gone a long way toward reclaiming it—vines, mosses, bromeliads, and even trees with long, snakelike roots crowded its crumbling steps and basked in the sun atop its templed crown. But the resurgent foliage hadn't yet been able to obliterate its man-made lines. No doubt about it: an undiscovered Mayan temple.

And *I* found it!

His heart raced with exhilaration. He hadn't been here a day and look what he'd discovered.

When was the last time human eyes looked on this spot? he wondered. A hundred, five hundred, a thousand years?

Mesmerized by the wonder of that possibility, he pushed through the undergrowth toward his find.

Passing a tilted, vine-covered column that he at first took to be a dead tree trunk, he was startled to see a pair of eyes peering out at him. As he cut away some of the vines for a better look, he realized that he'd found a Mayan stela, one of the carved stone pillars they set up around their public areas. This one appeared to be red sandstone; it stood a good eight feet above the ground, and probably had at least another four feet planted in the soil.

The parted vines revealed a frowning face, almost Asian in its flatness, wearing an elaborately carved headdress alive with gaping jaws and bared teeth. A snarling jaguar head jutted from where his chest should be. But the cold merciless eyes of that face unsettled him.

He moved on toward the pyramid—*his* pyramid—and started to climb its steps. The sound of rushing water was louder here and he hesitated. The exertion of cutting his way through to here had increased his thirst. Maybe he should find the river, then explore the pyramid.

The light suddenly faded and Will looked up. A dark billowing cloud had swallowed the sun where it had been poised above the trees. A deep rumble of thunder announced that Ambrosio's Chac was coming back for a return engagement.

Will looked longingly toward the boxlike temple atop the pyramid, but decided to postpone a peek inside. He didn't want to get caught out in the storm that was barreling this way.

If nothing else, he thought as he hurried back toward the trail, the rain will solve the thirst problem.

By the time he found the gully, the wind was bending the trees and shaking loose the remainder of the last downpour. The roaring thunder and lightning flashes filtering through the leafy canopy spurred him into a run. He made it to the Jeep just in time.

Will had heard of tropical rains but had never experienced one. There was no build up—one moment the storm was threatening, the next instant he was underwater. If the Jeep had been moving, he'd have sworn they'd driven into the Mesoamerican equivalent of Niagara Falls. The water battered the hood like a thousand angry fists, *pounded* the canvas roof with such force that Will cringed in his seat, fearing it would tear and he'd drown. A couple of minor rivulets ran down the inside walls from leaky seams, but nothing serious. He stayed dry, but he could see nothing but water through the windshield. His world had shrunk to this noisy little two-seat cubicle.

The storm raged for a good hour, then gave up and moved on, leaving Will in the dripping darkness. Night seemed to fall as quickly as the rain.

Will unsnapped the door and stepped out for a breath of fresh air. His boot landed in running water. The gully had turned into a stream.

Where the hell was Ambrosio? How long before he got back? He hoped nothing had happened to the little guy.

Will hopped back up on the narrow running board. At least the Jeep was clean now. He scooped some water off the canvas roof and drank it.

Swallowing accentuated the fullness at the back of his throat, reminding him of the ticking bomb within. He drank some more, then crawled back into the Jeep and buttoned it up.

So here he was, alone in the dark, with no idea of how long he'd be stuck here.

Might as well make the best of it, he thought.

He reached over the seat, unzipped his duffel, and extracted his laptop. Maybe he should start the journal of his adventure tonight. And maybe not. He wasn't sure he could resist the temptation to open this chapter with, "It was a dark and stormy night."

He decided to send e-mail first. He tapped out a message to Kelly, telling her he'd made it to wherever he was—he told her he was in Mexico—and that he was doing fine.

He plugged his satellite modem card into the PCMCIA slot and raised the little antenna. The Jeep's canvas top wouldn't hamper his uplink a bit. He'd been told that this was the cutting edge in computer communication and would work anywhere in the world. It had worked fine in Westchester, but this would be the real test.

It took three tries, but finally he managed to log onto his e-mail account via satellite. As he uploaded Kelly's letter, he saw that he had mail waiting for him—from Terziski. He downloaded that and read it immediately:

Doc—

Having trouble confirming Maya Quennell's CV. Discrepancies at her primary sources. Checking further. Will get back to you.
—Terziski

Terse and to the point. Too terse. Terziski seemed to think e-mail was like a telegram—he wrote as if he were getting charged by the word.

"Discrepancies at her primary sources . . ." What the hell did that mean? The detective hadn't come right out and said Maya was lying about her past, but that was certainly the implication.

Great. Will had left behind Western civilization to trek off with a woman with discrepancies at her primary sources. He hoped he heard back from Terziski before he got too deep into this . . . whatever this was.

But for now, might as well make the best of it.

He didn't feel like writing, so he zipped the laptop back into the duffel, then checked the fittings on the canvas top, making sure they were snapped shut. He was pretty well shielded from nuisance creatures, like insects and snakes, but what about predators? Were there any? He remembered the jaguar head on that stela. Hopefully none of them were about, or if they were, he hoped they'd avoid something the size of the Jeep.

Figuring sleep would speed the passage of time, Will pushed back the seat as far as it would go, got as comfortable as he could, and closed his eyes . . .

7

"Wha—?"

Will awoke with a start. He straightened in the seat. How long had he been asleep? And what had awakened him?

A flash of light and a not-too-distant bellow answered the second question. Another storm? Didn't Chac give up?

The rain hit then, drowning out the thunder as it attacked the Jeep with another mad cacophonous tattoo like automatic gunfire against its roof and hood. Will wouldn't have thought it possible, but rain from this new storm seemed heavier than the last. How could clouds hold this much water?

And then the Jeep moved.

What the hell?

Will grabbed the dashboard as the vehicle swerved to the right, bumped something, then swerved left and stopped with a jolt. He moved his leg and heard his boot splash. Reaching across to the driver's side, he found the light switch and turned it. The glow from the dashboard revealed nearly an inch of water on the floor, and more running in around the door flap. He pushed the flap open and gasped as water cascaded into the Jeep. A brilliant flash of lightning revealed little through the deluge, but enough to show water flowing all around. Flowing fast.

The gully had become a rushing stream. The rain alone couldn't account for all this. Only one explanation: the river, the one he'd heard but not seen, was overflowing its banks.

He pulled the door shut again, but the floor of the Jeep was now awash.

I should be all right if I sit tight, he told himself. After all, how high can it get?

As if in answer, the current lifted the Jeep and began to carry it along. Will felt his heart hammer against his chest wall as the little vehicle tilted left and then right.

Don't panic, he told himself, but remembering how these vehicles had been criticized for having too high a center of gravity did not help.

Moving sideways, the Jeep picked up speed until the driver side wheels caught on something and it began to tip.

"Oh, Christ!"

Will kicked out the passenger door and scrambled out. He landed in waist-high water. Through the lightning-strobed torrent he saw the Jeep tip about forty-five degrees, then hold. The current swirled around it, pushing at it, but whatever it had caught on seemed to be supporting it. But it was useless to Will as shelter. He had to get out of this water. He imagined snakes and maybe even alligators floating his way from the river . . .

Yes, he definitely had to climb a tree or find higher ground, but first . . . he reached back into the Jeep and found the machete. Good. At least he had a chance of self-defense with that. Now where?

The pyramid.

How far had he floated? Surely not past the trail he'd found earlier. Using the lightning flashes to guide him, he moved further downstream, trying to remember any landmarks he'd passed this afternoon, but it was no use; everything looked so different now.

Finally he spotted an opening in the brush but couldn't tell if it was the same one. He didn't care. He had to get out of this mini-river. He splashed up to the bank, but as he followed the trail, he sensed the water rising behind him.

Where the hell am I?

He almost cheered when the lightning revealed a recently hacked web of vines directly ahead. He scraped through as a particularly brilliant flash drenched the clearing in white light. Even so, he could barely make out the ghostly shape of the pyramid dead ahead. The rain fell even harder here in this open area, so hard he felt he might have to use his machete to carve his way through the cascade.

He splashed toward the pyramid. And the closer he got, the eerier it looked in the flashes. Almost forbidding. But he couldn't let that put him off. He needed a high, dry sanctuary against the rising water, and right now the temple atop this pile of stone was the only game in town.

He slowed as he hit the steps, picking his way by touch and an occasional flash as he climbed over the vines and tree roots, skirting the bushes. After a few minor stumbles and scrapes he made it to the dark maw of the temple—literally a maw, since the Mayas had carved the head of some sort of monster around the opening.

He stepped through and stood dripping in the darkness, reveling in simply being out of the rain. He looked around. The space measured ten by twelve at most, with an identical doorway in the opposite wall. Small, yes, but it was relatively dry. The roof leaks were minor. Those Mayas knew how to build.

It took him a moment or two longer to realize that he was not alone.

The smell was the first clue—the acrid scent of animal droppings. The rustle of leathery wings in the darkness above him was the confirmation.

Bats.

Will ducked into a cringing squat and looked up at the ceiling. He could see nothing there. But he definitely could hear their agitated wings and an occasional squeak. He guessed they were about ten feet above him in the narrow angle of the roof.

Lots of bats in the northeast were rabid. What about these? And weren't there vampire bats in this area of the world—the ones that sucked blood from cattle? Or was that in South America? He never should have canceled his subscription to *National Geographic*.

At least these bats were staying put up there in the dark.

"Let's make a deal," he whispered to the ceiling. "I'm not here to bother you, so don't bother me. Okay?"

He sidled over to a corner and crouched there with his back against the wall, watching the storm. The trees swayed and bent to impossible angles under the relentless onslaught of rain and wind. The clouds teemed with electricity, repeatedly lit from within by frantic flickers and huge, booming discharges as they pressed a billowing lid down on the clearing. Will had never seen a storm of such maniacal intensity.

He jumped as a sizzling bolt of lightning *cracked* into a palm at the edge of the clearing, exploding its crown in a multicolored fireworks display. He closed his eyes, clenched his teeth, and hung on, watching the jagged afterimage on his retinae as the immediate deafening boom of thunder shook the pyramid to its foundation. When he looked again, the palm was split down half its length and blazing fronds were pinwheeling through the air. The rain drowned the flames before they reached the ground.

That was when he realized with a jolt that he was sitting atop the tallest structure in an open clearing. This temple could be the next lightning target. In fact, it almost begged to be hit.

Have to risk it, he thought. He wasn't budging from this dry spot.

He glanced down the steps and thought he saw movement. At first he assumed it was just an effect of the flickering light, but a few seconds of scrutiny confirmed his first impression: something was moving down there—lots of somethings—and they were climbing this way.

And then another particularly bright flash allowed him to identify them.

"Oh, Christ!"

Rodents of all shapes and sizes—rats, mice, and other ratlike and mouselike things he couldn't identify—were scrambling over, under, and through the vines and roots to get away from the flood waters. He shrank back against the wall and held his machete before him, ready to fend off any that came too close.

But they didn't seem interested in the temple. They were diving into all the nooks and crannies, cracks and crevices in the pyramid's crumbling façade.

"Good," he said aloud. "Those are good places for you. Nice and tight and dark and dry."

But something else was happening. As the rats and mice were going in, other things were coming out: insects. A rippling wave of displaced beetles and spiders—some of them very *big* beetles and spiders—was scrambling toward the top . . . toward Will.

He drew his feet and legs back tight against his body and wanted to cry out in revulsion as they swarmed into the temple, a thousand tiny scuttling shapes flowing across the floor and crawling up the walls. Most avoided him but a few ran across his boots or bushed his arms. He shivered and twitched them away.

He'd always found nature fascinating, especially bugs and spiders, but they'd always been on a TV screen or on the far side of plate glass at the zoo. The knowledge that thousands of them were clinging to the stones above and around him was almost enough to make him bolt back into the rain.

But no. He'd been here first.

And then he remembered that bats thrived on insects. What if they went into a feeding frenzy, swooping against the walls, knocking the bugs and spiders onto Will . . . into his hair . . . down his collar . . . ?

His skin crawled as he quickly buttoned his collar.

"Everybody play nice," he whispered, glancing up to where the invisible bats hung. "Please. Just until the storm gives up and moves on."

Another day-bright flash revealed half a dozen new shapes scurrying up the pyramid steps. They moved like rats but were much, much larger.

Will groaned and tightened his grip on the machete. Now what?

As they rushed into the temple space, their feet clacked like tiny hooves as they danced about and shook the rain from their brown spotted fur. Ambrosio had pointed out one of these tailless furballs earlier. He'd called it a paca, and said they lived in burrows. Will was ready to bet all their burrows were flooded now.

"Welcome to the club," he said.

They shied away from him and clustered in a knot in an opposite corner.

"Who's next?" he said, half-jokingly, and then froze as he caught sight of a large swift sinuous shape moving his way up the steps.

Will knew immediately it was a big cat. And it was carrying something in its jaws.

Will had hung in through bats and bugs and pacas, but now, storm or no storm, it was time to leave. But before he could rise and move, the cat was in the doorway, statue-still on the threshold, staring at him. Fear gripped Will's pounding heart in an icy fist as a flash illuminated the black-ringed spots on its matted fur. A jaguar. He shifted the machete so that its point was pointed at the cat's throat.

And then he noticed the squirming bundle dangling from its jaws: a cub.

The jaguar bent and released the cub. As it rolled to its feet and shook itself, the mother tilted her head, spread its jaws, and let loose something between a growl and a hiss. Whatever it was, the sound stampeded the pacas back into the storm. Will very much wanted to be with them, but he couldn't run now, didn't even dare move other than to extend the machete point a few inches toward the cat. He wanted to tell her to stay back, but all his saliva had left his mouth, most likely gone to his bladder which wanted very badly to empty—*now*.

Without another sound, the jaguar turned and ducked back into the storm.

Will huddled against the wall, debating whether he should make a run for it. The big cat hadn't attacked him or even gone after the pacas. She seemed to have other things on her mind.

He caught strobe-effect glimpses of the cub as it circled about, sniffing the temple floor. It moved toward him, sniffed his boot, then began swatting at the laces with its paws.

"Get lost," he said, finding his voice again. But he didn't push the cub away. "I don't want your mother thinking I've been messing with you." He glanced down the steps and felt his insides tense again. "And speak of the devil . . ."

The big cat was back with a second cub. She licked the first one, almost knocking it over with her tongue, then gave Will another long look before ducking out again.

The two cubs began licking the rain off each other, and continued that until their mother arrived with a third cub. But this time she moved inside. She shook herself, spraying Will and most of the interior of the temple. He heard an agitated rustle close to his ears as the drops hit the insect horde clustered on the wall behind him.

Something dropped on his shoulder. He glanced right and saw a thick-legged hairy spider the size of his hand turning in a nervous circle on his shoulder. It took every last drop of will power to resist the instinct to scream, slap the thing away, and run howling into the storm. But he knew the big cat was watching him, and any sudden move would earn him a mauling.

And so, his skin rippling with revulsion, Will sat and watched as the big spider slowed its agitated movements. He prayed it would jump back onto the wall, but it seemed to like its new perch. It settled down two inches from his neck.

The jaguar, too, settled into a crouch and began grooming her cubs, drawing them one at a time between her huge paws and licking them dry. But all the while keeping an eye on the other two, and on Will.

Outside, the storm raged unabated. And behind the big cat he spotted the pacas creeping back into their far corner of the temple. The jaguar glanced at them once, then continued her grooming. One of the cubs, the curious one who'd been playing with Will's bootlaces, started over to investigate the new arrivals but the mother batted it back toward Will. So the cub came for his boot again.

Get away, little guy, he thought, projecting the silent words at the cub. Please don't draw any attention to me.

Apparently the cub wasn't telepathic. It began swatting at Will's bootlaces, but quickly seemed to tire of that.

Good. Go back to mama.

But the cub had other ideas. It hopped up on Will's thigh and tumbled into his lap. Will saw the mother's head snap up, heard a low growl rumble from her throat.

Fear sweat coursed down his body in rivulets. What did he do now? He sure as hell didn't want the mother coming over here and retrieving her little wanderer from his lap, but did he dare lift it and put it back on the floor?

And if he moved, what would the spider do?

The cub settled the crisis by curling into a ball and starting to purr.

Will and the mother stared at each other, but she was no longer growling. Lightning flashed in green eyes that reminded him of Maya's. She blinked at him, then turned back to one of her other cubs and continued grooming it.

And then Will noticed an odd sensation stealing through him, working toward his skin from deep within, spreading until it suffused and enveloped him.

Here he sat with a hairy horror on his shoulder, trapped between meteorological fury raging outside and imminent clawed death crouching just a few feet away, and yet he could not remember when he had last felt so at peace with himself, with the entire world.

No predators here in this tiny stone temple, he realized. We're *all* prey tonight. The storm and the river are the predators, hungry for us all. Tomorrow we'll go back to our ordained roles, but tonight, at this time, in this place . . . truce.

Gripping the feeling tightly to keep it from slipping away, he closed his eyes and clutched it to him. But he did not sleep. Oh, no, for then he'd lose the feeling, and he wanted to milk every last dram of peace from it. Who knew when he would feel this again, if ever?

Slowly, Will sneaked a hand from the machete handle and with one finger gently stroked the damp furball in his lap. It purred even louder.

He felt as if his head might float away.

PART TWO

Hidden Harmonics

1

I might have dozed off. I couldn't be sure because I'd lost all sense of time. I didn't remember the storm fading, but I did remember opening my eyes and looking out the temple doorway and seeing a translucent predawn sky turning the color of skim milk. The jungle's early risers were already calling and flitting from tree to tree.

The mother jaguar stood in the other doorway, staring out at the clearing. I wondered how that was sitting with the pacas, but then noticed that their corner was empty. So was my shoulder. My spider friend was gone. Couldn't say I'd miss him. I checked out the walls around me. A few roaches and smaller spiders still clung to the stone, but most of their many-legged brethren had cleared out.

I winced as needle-like claws dug into my thigh. The cub on my lap was awake and stretching its foot pads as it yawned. Finally it hopped down to the floor. It padded over to where its two siblings lay wound into a ball and jumped on them. In seconds they were rolling around on the stone floor.

The big cat turned then and approached them. It picked up one by the neck and headed for the door near me. As it passed, its green glare said, Don't even *think* about making off with one of these.

Never even crossed my mind, I thought back at her.

The remaining pair of cubs scampered to the doorway and started mewing after her. She picked her way quickly and gracefully down the steps and took off across the sodden clearing without a look back.

I decided this was an excellent time to make my exit. I sensed the magic worked by the storm and flood last night wearing off. Might be prudent to put some distance between myself and Mama Jaguar.

My chilled, wet joints creaked and protested as I uncoiled from my cramped corner and staggered to my feet. I felt like the Tin Man with a terminal case of rust. I groaned and arched my back, then stumbled to the opposite door—*away* from the jaguar cubs. Machete in hand, I made my way down the steps.

Except for the blasted palm and the squishy ground, the clearing and the pyramid seemed little changed since yesterday. The sky was rapidly growing lighter as I moved toward the trees. I placed myself behind a thick mossy trunk and peeked back at the pyramid. I spotted the mother jaguar already heading down again with another cub. I watched till she returned the third time.

"So long," I said when she exited with her last, and noted that my voice sounded unusually hoarse. The result of dehydration and a night sitting in bat guano? Or the tumor?

"Back to reality," I muttered as I stepped into the clearing. I looked at the temple and the surrounding circle of jungle.

This was reality?

My stomach rumbled with hunger. And I was thirsty as all hell. I never did find a coconut yesterday, but the jungle floor had to be littered with them this morning.

I rested my machete blade on my shoulder like a rifle and headed across the clearing. Yesterday I'd been so hesitant to enter the jungle. This morning was different. *I* was different. Somehow I felt Mesoamerica had already hurled its worst at me and I'd survived. I felt ready for anything.

As I'd guessed, no trouble finding freshly fallen coconuts. Opening them, however, was another matter. On the first two tries I split the damn things in half, splattering ninety percent of the milk across myself and the jungle. Ambrosio had made it look so easy.

On the third I got it right, chipping a small opening in the top. I drank greedily, gulping the cool, vaguely sour fluid as fast as my throat would allow, letting the excess run over my jaw. When had anything, even an ice-cold Rolling Rock after mowing the lawn, ever tasted so good?

I tried another and wrecked it, but was able to pop the top on the next. Then it was time to look for food. Not much meat inside these green coconuts, so I set about looking for one that had ripened a little more. I didn't have much luck on the coconut front, but I did come across a banana tree that had been knocked down by the storm. A bright green four-foot bunch lay in the brush, waiting for me.

I'd never eaten bananas this green but I wasn't going to let that stop me. The jungle was offering breakfast and I wasn't in any position to refuse. But as I started tugging at a couple of the bananas, a huge hairy black spider hopped out from within the bunch and scuttled toward me.

I jumped back and raised my machete. This was one scary-looking creature but I wasn't going to let it keep me from breakfast. My first instinct was to squash it with the flat of the blade, but I hesitated.

"Move on," I told it. "I had one of your cousins on my shoulder all last night. I'm up to here with spiders."

The thing didn't budge, so I gently slipped the point of the machete under its body. It jumped up on the flat of the blade and I quickly dumped it onto a broad leaf a foot or so away. It ran down the leaf and disappeared into the shadows.

"You need a new tree anyway," I called after it. "This one's shot."

I had to smile as I tore off a six-fingered hand from the bunch. I'd been here less than a day and already I was talking to bugs.

The bananas were puny and didn't have much flavor, but they

filled the void. I ate three, noticing a little difficulty in swallowing—nothing serious, but my gullet felt slightly narrower.

It's beginning, I thought with dismay. The traitorous tissue was extending its domain into areas where I'd be constantly aware of its presence. But I'd known this would happen, and I wasn't going to dwell on the inevitable.

I broke off another hand of bananas and took them with me as I made my way back to the clearing.

The sky was bright now, the sun cresting the trees and bathing the temple atop the pyramid—*my* pyramid—with golden light, but the rest of the clearing still lay in shadow. I wished I'd thought to bring a camera.

I headed back to the gully where I found red muddy water still running through it, but only a few inches deep. I made my way upstream to where I'd left the Jeep—at least where I *thought* I'd left it—but it wasn't there. I did find a freshly broken root jutting from the floor of the gully. This could have been what the wheels had caught on last night.

I got a queasy feeling in my gut, not so much from the missing Jeep—I was pretty sure I'd be able to find it somewhere downstream—but because of what I had *in* the Jeep. My duffel bag contained some extremely important equipment that I'd have no hope of replacing here in the wilds of Mesoamerica. And I wasn't thinking of my laptop.

I began splashing down the gully. How far could it have gone? And what if the duffel had washed out? It could be anywhere. The duffel was water resistant but not waterproof. And even if it remained in the Jeep, everything inside it could be water damaged by now.

I rounded a curve and there she was, upright and facing me, her rear bumper jammed into the curve of the bank. She was scratched, dented, filthy, and strewn with storm flotsam, but I thought her beautiful enough to kiss.

I slowed to a walk, gasping for breath—damn, I was out of shape. As I neared her, half a dozen screeching spider monkeys tumbled from the open side panel and scampered away into the trees. I picked up my pace. I knew from safari rides back home how much damage those little creatures could do to a car. I unsnapped the rear panel and sighed with relief when I saw my duffel, intact and still zippered closed.

But it was *wet.* My fingers shook a little as I yanked back the zipper and pawed through the clothing, toiletries, emergency medications, and sundry items inside. Everything seemed dry so far. Finally I found it—a small black leather case about half the size of the laptop. I unzipped that and checked the contents of the Ziploc bag inside. The two 250cc bags of dextrose and water were intact; the IV tubing and needles looked fine; and none of the ampoules of potassium chloride were broken.

I leaned my head on my arms and let go a deep sigh of relief. This was my escape hatch. If—I should say "when"—the tumor extended to the point where I could no longer swallow, or I was having too much difficulty sucking air past my swollen larynx, this was my exit ramp. Rather than let them cart me to some hospital where I'd be hooked up to IVs and feeding tubes, I'd brought along my own IV.

When it was time to check out, I'd empty the amps of potassium chloride into the D5W, hook up the tubing, hang the bag from a branch, stick the needle in a vein, and let it flow. The KCl cocktail would stop my heart muscle dead in its tracks.

Quick, clean, easy, and painless.

Well, relatively painless. I figured that high a concentration of KCl had to burn when it hit the vein, and I could count on some chest pain when my heart seized up, but nothing I couldn't tolerate for less than a minute. That was all it would take. A hell of a lot better and more dignified than the alternative. And best of all, *I'd* be pulling the plug, not the tumor.

I'd prevailed on Dave, as a last personal favor, to arrange to have my body shipped back to Bedford if I died down here. I hadn't told him that I fully expected the "if" to be a "when."

I heard a car engine somewhere far behind me. More relief. It could only be Ambrosio. I quickly zipped up the leather case and shoved it back into the duffel.

Now. How to play this? Should I be furious at being left alone in the jungle overnight in a storm, or be cool?

Curiously, I was not furious. I could have been killed, yes, but instead I'd had a once-in-a-lifetime experience that left me with a different take on the world, especially this part of it. Yesterday I'd been a complete stranger here. Now, although I was not by any means an integrated part of Maya's Mesoamerica, I no longer felt like an interloper. I felt tenuously . . . connected.

I'd come here for an adventure, and sure as hell, I was having one. So try as I might, I could find no anger in me.

But I wasn't cool either—I was going to be overjoyed to see Ambrosio. Damned if I wasn't ready to kiss his homely face when he showed up.

But I could *play* it cool. Very cool.

So when the other Jeep rounded the curve, I was lounging on the hood, back against the windshield, a machete through my belt, and a half-eaten banana in my hand.

Ambrosio jumped out of the driver side, and from the passenger side—Maya. Despite Terziski's "discrepancies at her primary sources," my heart gave a little tug at the sight of her. So she hadn't abandoned me in the forest. She wasn't Xtabay.

But though this Maya bore little resemblance to the woman I'd met back home, she was just as striking, if not more so. She'd plaited her hair into two long braids and was dressed in an ankle-length shift of coarse white cotton, embroidered at the neck and hem and cinched at the waist with a colorful cloth belt.

"Dr. Burleigh!" she said, hurrying toward me. "Are you—?"

"Care for a banana?" I said, holding up my leftovers. With food and fluid, my hoarseness had receded.

She slowed her pace and grinned. Those dimples appeared, and her jade eyes flashed.

Ambrosio began laughing, and rattled off a string of clicks, *shhshe*s, and hard consonants that definitely was not Spanish. Mayan maybe?

Maya was sauntering toward me now, hands on hips, smiling. "I was so worried about you, and yet how do I find you? Looking as if you have been on a picnic."

That smile. I was glad I could make her smile.

"Just because I'm the shining blind man in the fortress doesn't mean I'm not adaptable."

"Obviously this is true."

Over her shoulder I spotted a second man crawling out of the rear of her Jeep. He'd been cut from the same stuff as Ambrosio; looked like they even had the same dentist.

"Buenos dias," he said with a gilded smile.

"That is Jorge," Maya said. "He knows engines. He and Ambrosio are going to stay here and get this first Jeep going again while you and I travel on in the new one."

"Sounds good to me," I said.

I hauled out my duffel and carried it to the new Jeep. I waited for Ambrosio and Jorge to remove the tool box, oil cans, and gas jugs from the rear, then tossed it inside. I turned and found Maya in the driver seat, nibbling delicately on one of my bananas.

"Want me to drive?"

She shook her head. "Maybe later, but here I know the way better."

Ambrosio and Jorge waved as we drove off.

I watched Maya drive. She was relaxed, almost casual, and worked the standard shift like a pro. Her long legs pulled at the fabric of her shift as her bare feet worked the gas and clutch pedals.

"Is that a native dress?" I said.

"It's called a *huipil.* It's very comfortable."

"That and the braids make you look like you belong here."

"Thank you. In Westchester the braids would be seen as an attempt to look girlish. Here they are simply practical." She glanced at me. "And you . . . you look . . . different."

"Besides needing a bath and a shave?"

"Yes. Different inside."

I told her about last night. She nodded often as she listened, smiling now and again.

"You became closer to the Mother last night," she said when I was done. "Some of the walls of your fortress were weakened."

I didn't know about the Mother business, but I knew the night spent sitting in that ancient temple had taken me farther from my old life than the whole day of flying that had preceded it.

I began to wonder if that might have been Maya's plan all along: Have Ambrosio fake a breakdown and leave me alone overnight; a trial by fire, so to speak—or in this case, by storm.

I wanted to ask her, but didn't know how she'd react. She might take it as an insult. I decided to see how things went and ask her later. I might ask about the "discrepancies" in her CV then too. Or I might wait until I heard more from Terziski.

Right now, as we splashed along the green tunnel of the gully, I had another, more immediate question.

"Where are we going?"

"To find your first harmonic."

"Harmonic? What's that?"

"Do you remember the tines I used to survey your chakras?"

"Of course."

"We are going to find some for you and let you make them your own."

"Find? You make them sound like they spring from the ground, like mushrooms."

"They don't grow. They were fashioned, and then hidden away."

"By whom?"

"No one knows."

This was starting to sound like science fiction. "Okay, we find these tines, then what?"

"You will see."

"These tines," I said. "They aren't anything like crystals, are they?"

A tiny smile. "You have a problem with crystals?"

"I do," said, thinking of the mythology that had grown up around them. "But let me ask first. What do crystals mean to you?"

"The Mother forms them deep within her, putting sand and water under heat and pressure for millions of years, and then she pushes them to the surface. Some say they are her tears."

"You don't believe *that* do you?"

She shrugged. "I feel it is a bit romantic, but who is to say?"

"Do you believe they have mystical powers?"

"What do *you* believe?"

Remembering the crystals hanging in her office, I chose my words carefully.

"I'm not looking to offend you, Maya, but I've got real problems with that whole crystal business."

"You will not offend me. Ask—ask anything you want. I will tell you what I know. That is the only way you will learn, the only way blind Cecil will learn to see."

"I can question anything and everything? I can speak bluntly and you won't mind?"

"I insist."

"Oh-ho," I said, grinning. "You may regret that."

She returned the smile. "Yes, I am sure I will."

"Okay. Crystals. They're just rocks. All rocks except meteorites come from the earth—'the Mother,' as you call her. So why should crystals have more powers or healing properties than, say, slate? Or granite?"

"If you had to guess, how would you answer?"

"I'd say it was because they're prettier and make nicer jewelry than slate or granite, and therefore command a better price."

Another smile. "So, you are a cynic as well as a skeptic."

I shrugged. "You haven't been dealing with HMOs and the other zillion breeds of managed care companies like I have."

"No," she said. "Insurance companies would never approve of my methods."

"Yeah, well, they were never too crazy about mine either. I tended to ignore their guidelines. I can't tell you what it did to me to hear of their CEOs taking home millions of bucks a year—I read of one guy getting *eight* million in cash and stock one year—while the care and services their companies offered were cut to the bone. Make the patients crawl for days through a bureaucratic maze to get an antibiotic that's less than ten years old, but keep that bottom line where it does the most for the stock. And on the doctor side, build in disincentives to actually *treat* people. Squeeze the doctors, squeeze the patients so that some MBA can get a bigger year-end bonus, because God knows eight million isn't enough—he's got to have more. I know doctors saving lives every day who don't make one twentieth—one *fortieth* of that. And how many lives has this CEO saved?"

My voice was getting hoarse. I stopped and cleared my throat.

"You are very angry," Maya said.

"Yes. I am." I hadn't realized just how angry. Dealing with managed care companies was one part of my practice I didn't miss. "So maybe you can understand why I get an attack of cynicism when I see lots of money being made in medicine, established or 'alternative.' And believe me, somebody's making a killing on all those zillions of crystal pendants being sold because of their supposed healing powers."

"Yes, that is true. Wherever there is a need, profiteers are sure to rush in. But that says more about the sellers than what they are selling. Crystals are indeed rocks, but not 'just' rocks."

"Basically we're talking about quartz, right?"

"Yes. You have heard of a quartz radio, yes?"

"Of course."

"Have you ever heard of a slate radio or a granite radio?"

"Touché," I said.

She had me. No slate or granite or any other rock I could think of had piezoelectric properties.

Obviously she'd had this conversation before. How many times? Lots, I'd bet. She seemed so very comfortable with it. And with whom? I watched her long slim fingers on the steering wheel, the play of the muscles just beneath the skin of her forearms as she guided us along the gully, and wondered if she had a man in her life. And if not, why not? So much I didn't know about this woman.

"And can slate or granite rotate the plane of polarized light?" she said.

"Of course not."

"Then you will grant that quartz is not just another rock? That it has properties other than being 'prettier' which set it apart from other rocks?"

"Granted, but not necessarily healing properties."

She glanced at me, her expression serious. "Do you *know* that they do not?"

"No," I admitted, "I don't know much at all about this stuff. But I haven't seen any concrete evidence to convince me of any healing properties in quartz, and until I do . . ."

"You will go on doubting."

"Right. How can I do anything else? It's the way I've been trained. The scientific method. Double-blind randomized trials. I can't accept anecdotal evidence—you know, 'Aunt Sophie tried it and after one sip she threw away her hearing aids.' You've got to rule out placebo effect, investigator error, and prejudice. And the results have to be reproducible. That's the key."

"Then I suppose you must disbelieve much of what most people do believe."

"You've got that right. I don't believe in psychic hotlines, flying saucers, visiting aliens, astral projection, channeling, tarot, telepathy, spoon bending, clairvoyance, seances, remote viewing, reincarnation, astrology, aromatherapy, psychic surgery, perpetual motion, Genesis, Revelation, Kaballah, palmistry, phrenology, levitation, the Bermuda Triangle, Edgar Cayce, Jean Dixon, Immanuel Velikovsky, L. Ron Hubbard, the Loch Ness monster, and lots of other stuff I can't think of at the moment."

"I really do have my hands full with you, don't I, Wilbur Cecil Burleigh."

"I warned you."

"Surely you are the most skeptical man in the world."

"Oh, I doubt that," I said.

Maya hit the brakes, and as we skidded to a stop, she threw back her head and laughed loud and long. A wonderful sound, bursting from deep within her.

But what was so damn funny? And then I realized what I'd said and began to laugh along with her.

When was the last time I'd laughed like this, sharing it with another person? I couldn't recall. Not since the divorce, certainly, and probably not for a good long time before that. It felt so good to lean back and roar—at myself, of all things. What a wonderful release. I couldn't remember when I'd felt so alive.

For the first time in too, too long, I was having fun.

2

Eventually Maya climbed the Jeep out of the gully and headed uphill. The jungle didn't thin, it simply became slanted. The going got rougher as we bounced along a rudimentary trail. At one point we slowed to a crawl to negotiate our way past a pair of old huipil-clad women, each leading a burro-powered wagon.

We stopped where the ground leveled out in a narrow pass between a couple of the mountains. Maya had brought along some rice and beans wrapped in thick corn tortillas, and we ate them, washing them down with cool tea from a thermos.

After a bumpy ride through the pass, we made it to the other side of the mountains. It was drier here, and the trees seemed more coniferous, but it was just as green.

"Why travel all this distance for tines?" I said. "You seemed to have a nice collection back in Katonah."

"Yes, but they are mine. I am taking you to places where you can find your own. They will help you harmonize with the Mother."

"You're talking about a planet as if it's a person. The earth is a clump of stellar debris circling a ball of fusing hydrogen."

Maya shook her head. "The earth is a living thing, the All-Mother. Some call her Gaea, some call her Tellus, but by whatever name, she is alive."

"Sorry," I said, always careful about treading on someone's holy ground, "but planets are *not* alive."

"Maybe Mercury and Venus and Mars and the rest aren't, but ours is. When the living things on a planet reach a certain critical mass, the combined life force imbues the planet with a life of its own, separate from the creatures it nourishes. The planet itself becomes an entity."

I said nothing, just rolled my eyes.

"I know some things that you do not, Dr. Burleigh," she said with a touch of heat that brought a bit more French into her accent. I kind of liked that. "And this is one of them: Gaea is real, she is the All-Mother, *your* mother. Your mother loves you. She will heal you if you will let her."

I was struck by the sincerity and deep belief in her voice. But that wasn't enough. I could not accept her Gaea.

And I knew I was on her holy ground.

"Call me Will," I said to change the subject.

"No," she said. "I will call you Cecil."

"Forget it!"

"Yes," she said, smiling now. "You are Cecil until you learn to see."

Swell. I'd always hated that name.

Around us the trees were thinning enough to allow glimpses of the sun. From its angle I gathered that we were presently traveling northwest.

"All right," I said. "So we're going in search of these tines. What's so special about them?"

"They are hidden in four places, and the tines you will find in those places have not been touched by another living creature for ages. Once you take and hold one, it will become yours forever."

"'For ages,' eh? How come?"

"They are ancient, from another time, forged by another race. Their locations are secret. And even after you know the locations, the tines are not easy to reach."

I wasn't sure I liked the sound of that.

We wound along a sloping path until the trees abruptly disappeared, leaving us in the open.

"Here we are," Maya said.

I expected to see a clearing, but instead an open pit gaped before us. I got out and walked to the edge. It looked as if a giant angry fist had punched into the crust of the mountainside, leaving a rough hole about a hundred feet across. A meteor, maybe? Or just some sort of sink hole. I peered over the edge. Ragged sandstone walls dropped a good fifty feet to the sloping, sand-covered floor.

"You're going to tell me the tines are down there, aren't you."

"Only one of them. There's a little cave at the bottom that—"

"You really expect me to go down there?"

"You must. How else will you find your first harmonic?" She stared into the pit. "I was hoping it had rained here, but apparently the storms stayed on the other side of the mountains. This will make it more difficult."

More difficult? Not what I wanted to hear. I considered those steep walls and didn't like what I saw.

"Look, I'm not a mountain climber. There's no way I can make it to the bottom."

"You had almost no sleep last night. Do you not feel strong enough today?"

"I'm okay that way. I just—"

"Are you afraid of heights?"

"No. Not really."

"Good. Because we must stay on schedule."

"What schedule?"

"You must have all your tines before the full moon."

"What's the full moon got to do with it?"

"You will see. Come," she said, turning away. "Help me."

I followed her back to the Jeep and might have been more interested in the sway of her hips beneath her huipil if that pit hadn't been yawning behind me. I helped her haul a long coil of half-inch rope from under my duffel.

I grunted as I hefted it onto my shoulder. "How long is this?"

"Almost two hundred feet."

She pulled a cloth sack from the Jeep and together we returned to the edge. I dropped the rope near an ocote pine and peeked again into the pit. I felt my insides begin to constrict. How was I going to do this?

I licked dry lips. "Where's that cave you mentioned?"

"Straight down from here," she said. "Because the sand is dry, it is best to approach the cave from directly above."

"How many people do this?"

"Very, very few. It is a secret place."

"You've been down there?"

She nodded. "Many years ago."

"What's the problem with the sand being dry?"

"If you disturb it too much, it will start sliding into the cave mouth."

"And that's bad?"

"It will seal the cave until the next rain."

I took a deep, anxious breath. I didn't want to do this, but couldn't bring myself to tell Maya I was too scared to try. Especially since she'd already been down and back.

Male pride—it's a hell of a burden.

She began looping the rope around my waist.

"This will keep you from falling."

I liked that idea. Maybe this wouldn't be too bad.

She secured it with some sort of non-slip knot, then reached into her bag and brought out a flashlight and two pairs of sturdy-looking work gloves. She clipped the flashlight to my belt, then handed me the larger pair of gloves.

"To protect your hands on the climb."

I pulled them over my sweaty palms. It was hot out there in the direct sunlight, but that wasn't why my palms were wet.

Maya slipped into her own gloves, then freed a length of rope from the coil and wound it around the trunk of the pine.

"Ready?" she said.

No, I was not ready. Not even close to ready. Every neuron in my body, especially the more primitive ones in the hindbrain where self-preservation was the prime directive, screamed in protest. They thought they were still part of the old safe-and-sane Will Burleigh who'd never be part of a crazy stunt like this. But I'd left the old Will behind in New York. The new Will was damned if he wasn't going to live differently.

On the edge . . . very literally.

I can do this, I told myself. Maya did it. So can I.

Steeling myself against a rush of vertigo, I knelt on the edge and slipped my foot over. I found a toehold, paused for a deep breath, then lowered myself over and began my descent.

The first ten feet or so were rough going, and I was glad Maya had supplied me with gloves—the practice of internal medicine does not exactly prepare hands for clinging to rock. After that the wall sloped outward at a slight angle which made it easier to see where to put my feet.

Maya was leaving about two feet of slack in the rope. I learned that the hard way when my foot slipped and I lost my grip. I heard myself cry out in panic as I began to drop—but I fell only two feet before the rope snapped taught, cinching tight around my waist. I spun 180 degrees, bumping the back of my head against the rock.

"Are you all right?" I heard Maya call from above.

"Yeah," I said, dizzy and hurting as I frantically turned myself around and clutched at the sandstone. "Fine. Just a little slip."

I found a new perch on the wall, waited for my taching heart to slow, then continued down.

Somehow I managed to reach the bottom without catastrophe.

"I'm here!" I shouted.

I saw Maya's face appear over the ledge above. She smiled. "Wonderful. Stay right there while I send more of the rope down."

Almost immediately a seemingly endless length of rope began to snake over the rim and collect in a coil at my feet.

I looked around. The sandy floor of the pit sloped up and away from me at a good thirty-degree angle. The sand seemed to funnel down to a point a dozen feet to my right. I stepped away from the wall and spotted a dark crescent in the sandstone, maybe two feet high at its widest point. That had to be the cave mouth she'd mentioned.

I wiped my dripping face with my sleeve. Not a whiff of a breeze down here, and with sun directly overhead, the floor of the pit was like a giant wok.

The rope finally stopped falling, but a length still trailed up the pit wall. Maya's face appeared again.

"I have fastened the other end up here. Leave the rope tied about your waist."

"Why?"

"So you do not get lost in the cave."

Lost? How big was this cave?

"All right," I called. "You're the boss."

"Stay close to the wall as you approach the cave mouth," she said. "Disturb the sand as little as possible. And once inside, stay to the right. That path will take you to the tines."

"Gotcha."

"And remember, touch only one tine, the tine you will take and make your own. Leave the others alone."

With my back brushing the rock, I sidled along the wall to the mouth of the cave and peered inside. Dark as a grave in there. I went back and dragged the coils of rope to the mouth. The idea of an umbilical cord to the outside was looking better all the time.

I crouched and slid my feet toward the opening. Despite the heat, a chill of foreboding rippled over my skin at the thought of allowing myself to be swallowed by that hole. Who knew what was in there?

I pulled out my flashlight and aimed it through but the sun was too bright for me to make out any details.

Then I noticed the sand I'd disturbed starting to slide into the opening. I figured I'd better get moving before I disturbed some more. I entered feet-first on my belly.

More sand followed me inside and I noticed that the floor of the cave continued the slope of the pit. Maya had said to stay to the right and that was the way I rolled.

I sat up and brushed myself off, watching with mounting unease as the sand continued to slide into the opening, further narrowing the crescent of sunlight it admitted. Finally the sand slowed and stopped. I was relieved to see that I still had enough room to get out.

I closed my eyes to speed their adjustment to the darkness. At least it was cool in here, almost cold compared to the floor of the pit. When I opened my eyes again and played my flashlight beam along the walls, I saw that I was in a small chamber. A few large stalactites hung from the ceiling, but the sandy floor before me was smooth as baby's skin. No tracks other than my own. That was encouraging—I could safely assume that I wouldn't be running into any animals in here.

The chamber connected to a pair of tunnels; the one on the left was larger and ran steeply downward into yawning blackness. The one to the right had only a slight decline.

I started along the right. The ceiling of the tunnel gradually lowered until I was walking in a crouch, and then crawling on my hands and knees. It widened eventually into a chamber some twenty feet across—a *blind* chamber with a rutted ceiling only slightly higher than the tunnel's.

I squatted on my haunches and looked around, puzzled. I knew Maya had said stay to the right, and I had, but there was nothing here. Had I missed a side passage somewhere?

I was about to turn and go back when I noticed a darker area in the shadow behind one of the ceiling ruts. I crawled over for a closer look at what I assumed was a pocket recess and instead found a two-foot opening in the ceiling. I shone may flashlight inside and saw a narrow passage running upward at a steep angle for a couple of feet, then making a sharp turn . . . to where?

It looked like a tight fit. I wasn't claustrophobic, but the very real possibility of becoming wedged in that sandstone straitjacket, unable to move forward or back, broke my skin out in a clammy sweat.

I thrust my flashlight further into the opening and aimed the beam around the corner. The light that filtered back was brighter than I'd expected, and had a warm buttery glow . . . as if reflecting from a glossy surface.

I was going to have to crawl in. I didn't like the idea, but I'd come this far already. I simply told myself that if at any point I felt the passage was too tight, I'd retreat.

Keeping the flashlight extended before me, I eased myself into the vertical section and scraped my way up to the turn. I trained the light along the horizontal passage and blinked at a shimmering array of smoky yellow crystals, a huge pincushion of glittering six-sided needles not ten feet away.

I hauled myself up and belly-crawled the rest of the way on my elbows and knees with only a few scrapes and scratches. I thrust my head, arms, and shoulders into the three-foot-wide geode at the end of the passage and stared in wonder at the dazzling display around me. Hundreds of glittering golden spikes of all sizes jutted from every angle, like the ventricle of a crystal heart.

And jutting from the floor of that heart . . . four golden metal tines.

I stared in awe. Someone had fashioned these, hammered them into shape, then inserted them into the base of this huge, damn-near inaccessible geode. How long ago? And why? So that someone like me could come along ages later and find my "first harmonic"? It seemed beyond belief.

It seemed like sacrilege to take one, but I'd come this far and I wasn't about to come away empty-handed. I reached for the nearest tine and wrapped my fingers around it. Did I feel a surge of magical warmth arc up my arm? Did I feel a tingle of All-Mother energy course through me?

No. The only thing I felt was that I was somehow desecrating this beautiful display. But I had put myself in Maya's hands, and she'd sent me here to find them and make one my own.

I worked the tine free and started backing out. I had a bad moment when the rope around my waist bunched up and caught on the turn, but I wriggled around that and dropped back into the chamber below. I took another look at the tine, twisting it in the flashbeam and watching the golden reflections dance on the stone walls. Then I shoved it into a pocket and headed back the way I'd come.

I was feeling a little giddy as I followed the rope, looping it and carrying it along as I traveled. I'd done it. This wasn't like climbing Everest, or breaking the sound barrier, but for Will Burleigh, this was quite a feat.

When I saw the opening and the sunlight blazing through from beyond, I quickened my pace. I felt like a little kid finally getting his turn at Show and Tell. I wanted to show the teacher my prize.

I ducked into the opening and started to scramble through.

"Maya!" I called as I hit the sunlight. "I did it! I got one!"

"Will!" she cried from above. "The sand!"

I'd forgotten about the sand. It began to fall away beneath my feet, sliding into the passage opening, carrying me with it. I struggled to get free, but that only caused more sand to break loose and slide toward me, pushing me further. I was being carried back inside.

I cried out and frantically grabbed hold of the lip of the cave mouth but the sand kept coming, faster and faster in a miniature land-slide, filling in around me, choking the opening. I fought to keep my head free but the sand was flowing too fast. In seconds I was covered. Now I panicked and struggled like a madman—the cave entrance was filled; I couldn't move forward or back. I was trapped and I could tell by the increasing weight on my head and arms that more and more sand was collecting above me. No air! I was going to die!

And then I felt something snaking by me, rubbing against my left leg and arm—the rope. I grabbed at it, got a grip and held on with whatever strength was left in my air-starved muscles. My head banged and dragged against the upper edge of the cave mouth but I wasn't letting go. I felt myself pull free of the smothered opening, and then I was in the light, gasping lungfuls of air.

I let go of the rope and rolled to the side. I landed on my hands and knees, coughing and retching.

Suddenly I felt the rope tighten viciously around my waist. Next thing I knew I was being hauled into the air, kicking and struggling as I banged against the wall of the pit. But how? Maya didn't have the strength for this. Even if Ambrosio had arrived to help her, they couldn't haul me up at this speed. Did she have superhuman strength?

Abruptly I stopped rising and hung suspended thirty feet above the floor of the pit. I tried to call Maya's name but I still had too much sand in my mouth and throat. I looked up and saw her face reappear over the edge.

"Oh, my!" she said. "I went too far. Stay there! I'm going to pull you the rest of the way up!"

Stay there? What else could I do?

Seconds later, I began rising again. To avoid getting banged up even more than I already was, I grabbed the edge of the wall when I reached the top, and levered myself up and over.

The rope slackened immediately and I slumped face first onto the ground, panting and groaning.

I heard running footsteps approaching, and Maya's anxious voice.

"Will? Will, are you all right?"

I rolled over. Maya was looking down at me with a worried expression.

"Do I look all right?" I croaked.

"No. You are covered with sand and your scalp is bleeding."

"I feel worse."

"Is anything broken?"

I didn't think so. I struggled to my knees and Maya gave me a hand up to my feet.

"I'm okay," I told her. I wasn't, really. I hurt all over, my head was pounding, and my insides were jittering with adrenaline overload. "But that was too close. I damn near smothered down there."

"When I saw all that sand breaking free and sliding toward you, I didn't know what to do."

"You knew exactly what to do—and you did it. But how? One person, I don't care how strong, doesn't have the strength to . . ."

As I was speaking my gaze had been running along the length of the rope, following it all the way to the rear bumper of the Jeep.

"Oh," I said. "I see."

Quick thinking. Would I have thought of that if positions had been reversed? I felt a burst of warmth for this strange woman, and a little guilty that I'd doubted her motives for bringing me here. Even if she had discrepancies in her background, she'd just saved my life.

"Thank you."

"Do not thank me. It was I who endangered your life by sending you down there. I am so sorry this happened."

"I got careless," I said, reaching into my pocket. "I was kind of excited about finding this."

I pulled out the tine and handed it to her. She backed away with her hands flying out to the sides.

"No. Do not let me touch it. Do not let anybody touch it. That is your tine and only you may touch it."

"Why's that?"

"I will explain later. We will be spending the night not far from here. After we clean you up I will tell you."

Cleaning up—what a wonderful thought.

3

Another bumpy trek, shorter, downhill, and almost due west this time, until the all-enveloping jungle suddenly broke open into small, compact cornfields baking in the sun. A few hundred yards farther on we came to a tiny village of about ten or twelve huts with tall, peakcd thatch roofs. Maya stopped the Jeep on the outskirts, next to a long fence post strung with fifty or sixty corncobs, hanging in the sun to dry.

"Wait here, please," she said, "while I find us a place to stay tonight."

I remained in the Jeep and watched her enter one of the huts.

Peaceful here. Not far away a few chickens pecked at the dirt where two women dressed in bulky red blouses and long blue skirts worked outside one of the huts; each knelt before some sort of primitive loom. One end was attached to a wall, and the other was belted around the waist to keep it taught. I watched their quick agile hands manipulating the wooden rods and slipping the shuttle back and forth to weave a red fabric much like that of their blouses.

They glanced my way and toward the hut Maya had entered as they chattered. I figured I had to be the topic of conversation. Two dark-eyed, barefoot, laughing children, dressed only in ragged shorts, ran around from the far side of a hut and skidded to a halt when they saw the Jeep. Cautiously they approached to stare at the bloody-headed, sand-coated white man inside. When I smiled and waved, they dashed back to their mothers.

I did not pick up a welcoming feel. I was dzul, and that made me a little uncomfortable.

Maya returned a few minutes later.

"We can stay here," she said. "I know this woman. Her man is away and she will move in with her sister for tonight so that we can have her house."

"I don't want to put anyone out."

"I am paying her one hundred pesos."

I did a quick calculation: about twelve bucks. "Is that fair?"

"She asked for fifty," Maya said. She pointed to a well-worn path into the trees. "A stream is that way. You can clean up there while I help her move a few things to her sister's."

That sounded good. I grabbed my duffel and followed the path down a gentle slope. The palmettos and mahogany trees abruptly changed to willows at the water's edge. The stream looked to be about fifty feet across with a gentle current, its water the color of weak tea. To my left, a row of dugout canoes lined the bank. I moved upstream to my right until I found a spot where the bank was no more than a foot high. After checking the area for alligators and water snakes, I stripped off my filthy clothes, retrieved a bar of Lever 2000 from my duffel, and waded in.

The cool water was heaven-sent. I washed away two days of sweat and grime. I lathered up my hair and lacerated scalp; the wound stung as I washed out the dried blood and gently cleansed it. Then I rinsed my filthy clothes, dried myself off, and got into a fresh shirt and slacks. I didn't bother to shave.

When I returned to the village I found Maya standing in the doorway of the hut, smiling.

"You look like a new man."

I felt like one. I handed her a tube of bacitracin ointment I'd pulled from my medical kit.

"Could you put a little of this on my scalp?" I said. "It'll keep it from getting infected."

"I have something better," she said.

I didn't want to risk a homemade Mayan concoction. Better to stick with what I knew.

"I'd prefer this," I told her.

"If you wish. With my fingers?"

"Sure."

I bent toward her to place the top of my head within easy reach. Her touch was gentle and sent a pleasant chill down my neck as she applied the ointment.

"There," she said. "Now it is my turn to clean up." She motioned me inside. "Make yourself at home."

I ducked through the low doorway and stood in the dim interior. At least the roof was high. I looked around the single room. The walls were made of palmetto trunks lashed together and sealed with some sort of mortar; the thatched roof was a combination of grasses and palm fronds. To my left was the cooking area—a circle of stones formed the hearth; the flat metal top of a fifty-gallon oil drum served as a griddle; a variety of earthenware pots surrounded it. Next to that was some sort of altar with a picture of the Virgin Mary surrounded by offerings of flowers, incense, and what looked like tobacco.

Tobacco? I picked up a few strands and sniffed. Tobacco, all right. Fighting off the image of the Virgin Mary lighting a cigarette, I turned and checked out the rest of the hut.

A pair of hammocks stretched across the corners at the opposite end. And that was it. No table, no chairs, no shelves—the rest of the owners' possessions hung all about me on cords tied to the rafters.

What now? I had a sudden urge to return to the stream and watch Maya's ablutions, but overcame it. Where had that come from? Yes, I was sure Maya naked would be a wonderful sight, but I'd never been a Peeping Tom, and wasn't going to start now.

And on the subject of Maya, I wondered if Terziski had learned any more about her. I sat on one of the hammocks and pulled out my laptop. I typed a quick note to Kelly, telling her about my discovery of the Mayan pyramid but nothing about the stormy night I'd spent alone atop it. I made the satellite connection, uploaded the Kelly note, and found a note from her along with another message from Terziski.

Kelly told me Mom said hello and they were both glad I'd made it safely to Mexico—and now that I'd seen the place, couldn't I come back and start treatment?

"Sorry, Kelly," I whispered. "No can do."

I popped Terziski's note onto the screen.

Doc—

Lots of confusing data. Found a Maya Quennell listed with a philosophy degree in the Berkeley computer, but no academic record. Never registered in any (not a single one) of the core courses required for a philosophy degree. Berkeley folks were as puzzled as me. Looked like her name was just stuck into the computer.

Had a friend in France run a check in Paris. Found an Andre Quennell who worked as a journalist for *Paris-Soir* in the twenties and thirties. Found a record of a Maya Quennell at the Sorbonne, but get this: she graduated in 1938!!! (Has to be her mother.) Don't know anybody in Algiers where she says she was born, so can't help you there. But am going to take a good look at that protest arrest back in 1972. (I know she's too young, but how many Maya Quennells can there be in this world???)

Will be in touch.

—Terziski

Baffled, I reread the message twice, then stowed the laptop away. I lay back in the hammock, staring at the tools and utensils dangling above me like some giant mobile, and tried to make sense of this.

If Terziski was right, Maya's Berkeley degree was a fraud. But why lie about a degree when she didn't need one to be a New Age alternative "healer"? I couldn't find a rationale.

And if her degree was bogus, what else was she was lying about?

As I swung gently back and forth, I felt my eyelids begin to droop.

No sleep last night . . . climbing walls and crawling through caves today . . . I was bushed.

The chorus of uneasy questions swirling through my brain tried to keep me from dropping off.

They didn't have a prayer. . . .

"Wake up."

I opened my eyes to find Maya standing over me, gently jostling my shoulder.

"Time to eat. I cooked in another hut so as not to disturb you."

I appreciated that. Thoughtful, beautiful, resourceful—and she cooked too. How had she managed to remain unattached?

I swung my legs to the side and almost dumped myself from the hammock.

"Easy," she said. "They take some getting used to."

"I'll have to be careful during the night."

I stretched and glanced at my wrist, but I'd left my watch in the duffel after cleaning up. Through the door I could see that the light was fading. How long had I been asleep?

"What time is it?"

"Dinner time."

"Great," I said and let my annoyance show. "I ask where I am, I'm told 'Mesoamerica.' I ask the time, and it's 'dinner time.' Why can't I get a straight answer?"

I realized I was overtired and cranky, like a child who's just been awakened from a nap, but all this indirection coupled with Terziski's latest e-mail had me on edge.

Maya handed me an earthenware bowl filled with something steaming and spicy-smelling.

"It is dinner time in Mesoamerica," Maya said, a small smile playing about her lips. "What more do you need to know?"

"How about the name of the country, dammit. If I'd known you were going to be so mysterious, I'd have brought along one of those GPS doodads."

She seated herself crosslegged on the dirt floor near the door, next to a plate of tortillas.

"And what good would that do you?"

"I'd know my latitude and longitude to the second."

She looked up at me. "I repeat: What good would that do you?"

"I have a thing about knowing where I am. Whenever I've traveled I've had to have maps. Annie and Kelly used to call me a 'map nerd.' I suppose I was. I'd get to a city and immediately buy a street map and locate our hotel in relation to the major thoroughfares and landmarks. It made me feel secure—something I'm not feeling right now."

Maya was unimpressed. She patted the spot on the floor on the far side of the tortillas.

"Sit and eat."

With my knees creaking in protest, I grumpily assumed the position. Outside, the village was quiet—no children or chickens about, and the two weavers apparently had quit for the day. The wisps of wood smoke and the rich smells of cooking food wafted among the huts.

"What am I eating?" I said.

"Corn and beans in black chili sauce."

I spooned some into my mouth. Spicy but flavorful—the chili didn't overwhelm the beans and corn. I swallowed with a minimum of discomfort—the warm, moist mix slid down fairly easily.

"Delicious," I said. "But is this Mexican food, or Guatemalan, or Belizian, or what?"

"It's Mayan," she said.

I must have looked ready to scream in frustration, so she went on, speaking quickly, fire growing in her voice.

"I do not recognize the artificial borders that have been imposed upon my people's land. This is Mayaland, and it stretches from the tip of the Yucatan Peninsula down through the illegal and criminal states of Mexico, Belize, Guatemala, Honduras, and El Salvador. This is the land of the Maya nation, but these other so-called nations have usurped it. For centuries they have sought to destroy the Maya, using my people as either cannon fodder, scapegoats, or target practice, stealing our land, burning our crops and villages, raping our women, and slaughtering our men and children." She fixed her blazing green eyes on me. "So please do not ask me again what country you are in. The answer will always be the same: Maya country."

I ate in silence and let her cool. Obviously I'd touched a nerve. She had always been so calm and in control. Here was another side, an intensely passionate side. I found this little peek behind her façade oddly exciting.

I ate slowly. I had trouble getting the tortillas down unless they were slathered with chili sauce, so I stuck mostly to the mix.

"Fair enough," I said finally. "When people ask me where I've been, I'll just say, 'Maya country,' and let them figure it out."

A small smile as she stared out the door and nodded.

I said, "But you don't look like any of the Mayan women here."

This was obvious—she stood a good six to eight inches above the tallest Mayas—and I knew the reason, but I wanted her to tell me. I was testing her, I guess. She didn't know that I'd done a background check on her. I wanted to see if she'd tell me the truth.

"I am only half Mayan. My father was a French journalist who traveled here on assignment. He met my mother, they fell in love, and he took her back to Europe."

"You were born in Europe?"

"No. Algiers. Another of my father's assignments. It was his idea to name me Maya. My mother did not like the idea, saying it's the name of a people, not a person. But my father so loved the Mayas and the name that she finally gave in. He led an exciting life, my father. During the war he joined the French resistance. He worked with Albert Camus on the underground paper, *Combat*."

I was feeling a bit guilty now for testing her—this jibed with everything I knew. But the matter of the questionable Berkeley degree hung over me like a sword. I tried an oblique approach.

"How did you get into all this New Age stuff? I mean, was it part of your education in Europe?"

She laughed. "Hardly. There is nothing the least bit 'new' about what I do. It is ancient. I learned from my mother. We traveled back and forth often to visit her family."

"Did you ever have formal schooling? You know, college and the like?"

"I was educated all over the world, but it was here in Maya country where I learned the things that matter most."

Was she avoiding the question, or simply giving what she thought was a relevant response? As I was searching for a way to home in on the subject of higher education in the U.S., she took my empty bowl and moved back toward the hearth.

"More?"

I shook my head. "That was plenty. Thank you."

As she set the bowls down, I felt a tremor run through the ground, and heard, rather than felt, a low-pitched rumble. I'd never been in an earthquake, but I was sure the earth had just shifted under me. I turned and saw Maya standing in the center of the hut, still as a heron, her head cocked, listening.

"Was that—?" I began, but she cut me off with an abrupt wave of her hand.

I waited. Finally she relaxed and returned to my side. "Yes. That was an earthquake. A tiny one. They are common here. It is gone now."

"Nothing to worry about then?" I had visions of all these tools and utensils raining down on us from the ceiling.

"No. We are safe." She frowned. "I just hope . . ."

"Just hope what?"

"It is nothing. Show me your tine."

"It's in the duffel."

She looked concerned. "Oh, no. You must always keep it with you. Please bring it here."

I struggled to my feet and retrieved it from the duffel.

"I washed it," I said, holding it out to her, watching the firelight dance off the golden-hued surface.

"It is beautiful," she said. "And it is good that you washed it. That is your earth tine."

She kept her hands folded in her lap, and then I remembered what she'd said about not letting anybody else touch it. As I sat again, I plucked its pointed tip and listened to its hum, watching the light dance on its shimmering triangular surface. I wondered what it was made of. Too light for gold.

"What kind of metal is this?"

Maya shrugged. "I do not know. Each of the tines you must find is made of a different metal, metals I have seen nowhere else."

"What am I supposed to do with it?"

"Keep it always on your person, even when you sleep."

"That could get a little uncomfortable, couldn't it?"

She gave my poor attempt at humor just the amount of attention it deserved: She ignored it.

"Your tine needs to be near you, to imprint the unique wavelength of your personal energy."

"Energy?" I said. "What kind of energy? I hear people talking about energy all the time, like they're a microwave oven or something, or a battery that's got to be recharged every so often."

"The energy of your life force," she said. "It is generated in every cell of your body. Every living thing radiates energy; it creates an aura around them. Each of your tines must become attuned to your energy, so that it can harmonize with it. Your earth tine there will provide your first harmonic."

"My first harmonic," I said, turning it over in my hands. "Is it something I'll hear, like the tone when I pluck it?"

"No. It will be something you feel. You will know when it happens . . . it will be very much like the spiritual harmony you experienced atop the pyramid on your first night here, only far more intense."

More intense than that? I didn't know if I could handle that.

"You mentioned four tines, so can I assume that each of the tines will find their own harmony with me?"

"Yes. There are four tine harmonics, and one other. The most important of all: the Fifth Harmonic.

"Where's that come from?"

"From Gaea, from you, from everything. It is almost impossible to explain to someone whose third eye is blind. Do not concern yourself with the Fifth Harmonic now. Concentrate on the first. Let your earth tine find its harmony with you so that it can release to you what is stored within it."

I held up the tine and let it reflect the dying light of day.

"And just what exactly is stored within this baby?"

"A tiny droplet of the Mother's power, Cecil."

"You called me Will earlier."

"That was because I feared for your life. You are still Cecil. And let us not get off the subject of the power the All-Mother can store in that tine, a power you doubt."

"That's because I've never had any contact with your All-Mother, your Gaea."

She shook her head—sadly, I thought. "Yes, you have. Every day of your life. But you are blind to it, unaware behind your walls." She sighed. "The Mother wants me to heal the wounded healer, and to truly heal you, I must do more than heal your body. I must heal your mind and spirit as well."

There, I thought, is a tall order.

"And you think these tines will do that?" I said.

"If you let them, if you do not build more walls against them they can open your mind and free your imprisoned spirit, allowing you to rediscover your connection to nature and the divine."

Ah, if only something could do that . . .

I tightened my grip on the cylindrical handle of the tine and plucked again the wavy triangular head.

Harmonics . . .

I had no hope of a cancer cure, but I was open to finding a new way to look at the world in my final days. I'd give it a shot—that was part of the adventure—but I didn't see much chance of a spiritual awakening in my short future.

At least I'd be spending those days with a fascinating woman in a fascinating land.

I gave her my most innocent smile. "You've got your work cut out for you, don't you."

"Yes," she said, but didn't return the smile. Her expression became grimmer. "And I pray I am equal to the task."

4

I awoke to the sound of an angry voice—a male's, and not Ambrosio's. I looked across at Maya's hammock. In the early dawn light it hung limp and withered like an empty cocoon.

I rolled over in my own hammock and felt a jab in my flank. The tine. At Maya's insistence I'd stuffed it inside my shirt before sleep. It was warm against my palm as I pulled it out. I squeezed its handle, waiting, wanting to feel something different about it, about myself.

Nothing. Just a piece of metal.

I left the hammock and shoved the tine into a pants pocket as I padded to the doorway.

I couldn't find the sun, but the clear sky was bleaching to the east. A dozen feet away, a little Mayan man in a white shirt and loose pants was gesticulating angrily at Maya. His eyes were level with the base of her neck, so he had to tilt his head back to look at her.

I didn't know what all his glottal stops and *shhhe*s meant, but I had no doubt that he was angry. Maya was nodding, trying to placate him in the same tongue, but he wasn't having any of it. In fact, it only seemed to make him angrier.

Responding to an instinctive protective urge, I took a step forward. Maya spotted me and made a surreptitious *it's-okay* gesture with her hand.

I looked around and saw the shadowy figures of other villagers standing in their doorways, watching the contretemps. Then I noticed two other men standing off to my right. I looked closer and recognized Ambrosio and Jorge, and behind them, the other Jeep. I sidled over to Ambrosio.

"What's the problem?"

The little man leaned closer. "He is the man of the house you are staying in. He is very angry that you and Maya slept there."

"What's wrong? Not enough money?"

"No. He is saying that there is not enough money in the world to make Maya welcome in his house. And worse, she brought a Yankee dog with her." Ambrosio touched my arm apologetically. "Ambrosio does not say these things—only translates."

"I understand," I told him. "What else is he saying?"

"He says his home is now permanently tainted and he will have to burn it."

Tension thickened the air around me.

"Is he nuts?"

"I think he is big talk, putting on a show for his neighbors. He is even blaming Maya because his wife bears no children."

"Better than blaming himself," I muttered, then remembered what Ambrosio had said on my first day here: Some of the locals call her "*bruja*"—witch.

"He is also calling her a 'half breed,'" Ambrosio said.

And now I felt my anger mixing with the tension. The little jerk had no right to talk to her like that. I wanted to come to her defense but didn't speak the language. I could guess how Maya felt. She'd been so deeply angry last night about the centuries of depredations against *her* people, and here was this strutting little cock of the walk telling her she didn't belong.

Finally the man made a series of violent pointing gestures toward the end of the village—undoubtedly a demand that she hit the road—then stomped off toward one of the huts.

Maya walked over to us. She was dressed in a rough cotton blouse and cut-off shorts.

"We must leave," she said in a low, thick voice. She didn't look directly at me, so I couldn't read her expression in the dim light, but she sounded on the verge of tears. "We were only staying here this one night anyway, but we must leave immediately."

"No problem," I said, wanting to put her at ease. "I'm wide awake and ready to go. I'll stow my stuff in the Jeep."

"No," Ambrosio said. "No Jeep for you. Boat."

"Boat? Why a boat?"

"We take the river from here," Maya said. "We cannot reach the next tine by road, and it is too far to walk. Ambrosio will drive west and meet us later near the water tines."

"The river," I said. I'd never been much for boats. Lots of the other doctors I knew had cabin cruisers and sailboats and sport fishers, but the charm had always eluded me. "What kind of boat?"

"I bought one of the village dugouts yesterday."

Swell, I thought. A dugout to me was little more than an overweight canoe, powered by paddles. My back was already stiff and sore.

"Downstream, I hope."

That managed to elicit a tiny smile from Maya. "Yes. Downstream all the way."

"Good. Let's get going."

As I carried my duffel down to the stream, I worried about fitting it into a dugout canoe. But I was determined to find a way to take it along. No way was I going to be separated from my little Kevorkian kit.

I needn't have worried. The dugout was a big one, hand hewn from a twenty-foot cedar log, and back-breakingly heavy. It took the four of us to slide it from the bank into the water. The dugout easily accommodated my duffel and Maya's, plus a pair of sleeping bags and a cooler Ambrosio produced from the rear of the Jeep.

Maya took the rear position, I climbed in near the bow; our gear lay piled between us. A push from Jorge and Ambrosio, plus a few swift strokes from our paddles, and we were off.

We didn't have to work hard to keep moving. Maya used her paddle as a rudder to steer us to the center of the flow where the current did the rest. I dipped my paddle regularly, but it was more for show than anything else; the stream carried us along at an easy pace.

Behind us the sky glowed rose and gold as the sun clawed its way toward the tops of the dense tree walls lining the banks. Monkeys chittered in high-pitched voices as they scampered from limb to limb, bright green and red birds glided overhead, herons stood statue-still in the shallows, while kingfishers poised on the low branches, studying the flow, ready to lunge at anything that moved below the surface. Around us the water lay smooth and glistening, with only the faintest hint of a ripple—a mirror made by a glazier who hadn't quite got it right yet—to betray the presence of the current.

I glanced back at Maya. She was staring over her shoulder at the village as it disappeared around a bend in the stream. I admired the long slopes of her quadriceps running the length of her lean muscular thighs, saw them tighten and roll under the smooth brown skin as she knelt in the stern.

When she turned toward the front again, I saw the hurt in her eyes.

"Why was that man so angry?" I said.

"Because I am half dzul. The people in that little village are pure Mayan. They are very proud that they have not allowed their line to be tainted with dzul blood."

"Back where I come from we call that racism."

She sighed. "In a textbook sense, I suppose it is. But here in Maya country, it is different. Here they do not let bygones be bygones. They do not forgive, and they never forget."

"The injustices you were talking about last night?"

"Yes. But the centuries of slaughter are nothing compared to the devastation wrought by the diseases the dzul brought with them from Europe. Ninety percent—this is not an exaggeration, Cecil—nine out of every ten Mayas died in the plagues that stalked Mesoamerica during the sixteenth century. We lost our priest classes, our royal families, our daykeepers, our finest minds. Our towns became mortuaries. The raw number of dead among the Aztec, Incas, and Mayas is estimated at somewhere between forty and fifty million souls."

She paused, perhaps to let that sink in, perhaps to hear how I'd react. I was speechless.

She went on: "The Aztecs and the Incas had already been defeated militarily by then. The conquistadors had conquered them with their guns and swords, but the Mayas remained unbowed. The invaders needed the microbe as an ally against the Mayas."

Now that I thought about it, I remembered reading about the fall of Mexico City, and how, further south in Peru, Cortés or one of his fellow armor-plated barbarians had held the Inca king for ransom. But I knew nothing about the fall of the Mayas.

"We did not have a single king or a central royal city," she said. "We were scattered throughout Mesoamerica in dozens of self-contained pockets, much like ancient Greek city-states. There are still twenty different Maya languages. We were a hydra of a nation—chop off one head and the rest remained alive and well. That was our strength, *and* our great weakness. Our many city-states could not find a common leader to unite them and drive off the invaders. Or if such a man existed, he was taken by the plague before he could rise to power. By 1620, when your Pilgrims were landing on Plymouth rock, my people and their civilization had been reduced to an empty shell."

"'My people,'" I said. "It didn't look to me like that bantam-weight bully back there includes you in his version of 'my people.'"

"No. The women accept me but the men do not. The memories of the invasions, the old slaughters, the new slaughters, the Caste War have been passed on from father to son. The blood debt remains fresh. And the fact that I do not stay here in Maya country, that I shuttle back and forth between the land of the dzul, especially the U.S.—"

"The U.S.? We never invaded Maya country."

"Of course you did. With *Frutera*."

"With Who-whata? What are you talking about?"

"Frutera—that was what we called your invading army. Or sometimes 'the Green Octopus.' You probably knew it as the United Fruit Company. It tried to buy up most of Mesoamerica, or at least all those areas that could grow bananas. It controlled the railways, it rigged elections and maneuvered puppets into the presidential palaces. Where do you think the term 'banana republic' comes from? But when Jacobo Árbenez decided he wanted to give some of the uncultivated land back to the natives, Frutera called on its allies in the U.S. government. The CIA was sent in to arrange his overthrow."

"Oh, come on. Everything that goes wrong in the world gets blamed on either fluorocarbons, El Niño, or the CIA."

"This time it is true. John Foster Dulles was Secretary of State then. He was also a major shareholder in United Fruit. The head of the CIA was his brother Allen. Árbenez was labeled a communist, CIA-trained rebels overthrew him, and the disputed land went back to Frutera."

I didn't know enough of the political history of the region to argue with her. And I wasn't sure I wanted to. The story had an ugly and familiar ring to it.

"Mesoamerica has been in political turmoil ever since," she said. "Contras or Sandinistas, left wing or right wing, my people wind up either at the wrong end of the gun or in displacement camps. Somehow we always lose."

I turned and looked at her. "And where do you wind up?"

"In between," she said. "Always in between. Sometimes I am welcomed as a sabia—especially in places where I have healed. In other places, when something bad has happened after I have passed through, I am blamed, and from then on shunned as a wicked bruja. But even in places where I am welcome, I am not completely accepted. Always I exist one step removed. This is to be expected in someplace like Westchester. But even in my mother's village, I am an outsider." Her eyes glistened. "Nowhere is home."

I could have said something about everywhere being home if you believed in Gaea, but turned back to my paddling instead. She was hurting. Until this moment, I had perceived Maya as someone serenely self-contained, supreme mistress of her own skewed reality. But I'd just been allowed a glimpse into the heart of a very private woman, where all her vulnerabilities dwelt. I felt strangely privileged.

I wondered how I'd feel in her place. Here I was a born-and-bred American, a U.S. citizen, a licensed member of a respected profession, firmly entrenched in the social and economic fabric of my society. But Maya belonged nowhere. She spent her life adrift in a hazy no-man's land between cultures and races and nations. Even her belief system—what little I knew of it so far—lay outside the established safety zones of the major religions. How terribly *alone* she must feel at times.

I felt sorry for her. And I admired her too. Despite the pain it had to cost her, she wasn't giving in an inch. She wasn't hiding who she was, she wasn't backing off from her beliefs. Gutsy.

As we paddled on in silence, passing an occasional tiny village, I noticed a number of logs floating in the water near a sunny bank to my left. I was about to ask who'd cut them when a pair of eyes opened on one and it wriggled away from the others toward deeper water. I kept a close eye on it, wondering if it was going to come our way.

Maya must have been watching me. "Don't worry," she said. "It won't bother us."

"Crocodile or alligator?" I said.

"Alligator."

I jumped as I caught a flash of movement to my right—an eight-inch lizard was running across the surface of the water. It darted away from the bank, dipped its head to snatch something from the surface, then looped back to shore.

"Did you see that?"

"Jesus Christ," Maya said.

"My sentiments exactly."

"No-no!" she laughed. "They call that a Jesus Christ lizard. It got the name—"

"—because it walks on water," I said, getting the picture.

What a fascinating place. An endless parade of wonders. Why hadn't I done this before? Why had I waited until I was dying to experience the magic of this planet?

The stream widened, then joined another to create a wider channel that had to qualify as a river. The dugout rocked back and forth in the turbulence of the merging currents.

"Please don't tip," I whispered, remembering those alligators.

Maya had everything under control, however, steering us surely through the roiling waters with the apparent ease of skill born of long practice. We were moving considerably faster now, and the banks were farther away, at least fifty feet to either side. The current in this anonymous river—I didn't bother asking Maya its name—was strong enough to allow me to rest my paddle across my knees and become a passenger.

My watch was still in the duffel so I couldn't be sure, but it seemed to me that we traveled this way for hours, passing more villages and an occasional native boater who waved as he fished the river. The sun had climbed high above us; if not for the cooling effect of the river, we'd have been baking in its relentless glare.

Eventually we came to what at first seemed to be a small island. Maya steered us along its right shore. Only then did I realize that the river split here, and that we'd chosen the lesser tine of the fork.

The current slowed. Overhead the trees reached for each other like star-crossed lovers stretching to hold hands. Maya steered us leftward, out of the central flow and into blessed shade. Soon we were barely drifting. I lifted my paddle to begin pushing us along, but Maya stopped me.

"Let us rest a minute."

I looked back at her. Her face and legs glistened with a sheen of perspiration. Strands of hair too short to reach her braids framed her face in fine damp ringlets.

"Whatever you say," I told her. "You've been doing all the work."

She wiped a forearm across her brow. Her cheeks puffed as she caught her breath. She smiled, ruefully.

"I have been away too long. I am getting soft."

She opened the cooler and removed two bottles of water. She tossed me one and I took a long grateful pull on it. The first swallow was tight, but then my throat loosened up and I guzzled the rest as we drifted.

As Maya sipped hers she glanced up and pointed. "Look. A quetzal."

I followed her point and saw a parrot-like bird sitting on a palm branch. Its head and back were green, its belly a bright red, but no parrot I'd ever seen had tail feathers like this—vibrant green and running easily twice the length of its body.

"They were prized for their tail feathers. No self-respecting

114

Mesoamerican priest would be seen without a ceremonial headdress ablaze with quetzal feathers."

I was staring, captivated by the colors, when something hissed and rustled in the willow branches directly overhead. I shrank to my right and looked up, expecting a snake. I had a nightmare flash of a giant anaconda uncoiling from a branch and wrapping me up in a fatal stranglehold. Instead I saw a five-foot ring-tail iguana sticking out its tongue at me.

Maya laughed. "Do not worry. He does not eat people."

I stuck out my own tongue at the lizard as we passed. And then I caught a whiff of a sharp odor. I turned my head this way and that, sniffing the air.

"You look like a bloodhound," Maya said.

"What's that smell?"

"You don't recognize it?"

I sniffed again, detecting a sulfurous component. "No."

"It is fire and brimstone."

"Does that mean we're headed for hell?"

"It means we are nearing the place of the fire tines."

"Why does that not make me impatient to move on?"

She dipped her paddle and began stroking the water. "Now you may paddle."

The current slowed further as the stream widened again. No villages along this stretch. The sulfurous odor thickened in the air. We came to a curve, and as we followed that to the right, it opened into a wide lake, tranquil and blue, like an aquamarine embedded in a lawn. Low over the serene surface, a sulfurous haze undulated like a muslin shroud. And beyond the verdant rim of jungle towered a ring of black cinder cones.

A volcanic lake, either a water-filled crater or a basin between the cones. More likely the latter since the water was cool to the touch. I gawked, utterly taken with the beauty of the scene.

"Oh, damn," I heard Maya say behind me.

It was the first time I'd heard her curse. The word seemed almost obscene in this ethereal setting. I turned and looked at her.

"What's wrong? All we need are some monks and a city and we'll have Shangri-La."

"The lava is flowing," she said, pointing.

I followed her pointing finger to a plume of smoke and steam rising from the far shore, feeding the haze.

"Is that bad?"

"It can be." She pointed again. "There, to the left. We will land the boat there."

She was pointing to a break in the trees and what looked like a beach about two hundred yards this side of the steam plume. I bent my back to the task. No current here to help, and no more shade. I was panting and drenched with sweat by the time we made the shore.

The dugout nosed against the black pock-marked volcanic rock that sloped into the water. I jumped out and pulled the weighty bow as far up as I could.

At least it was shady here.

Maya brought the cooler to shore where we sat on the rocks and finished the rice and beans left over from dinner. I noticed that I was having a little more trouble swallowing the solids than last night. I didn't even bother trying a tortilla.

"You are having difficulty?"

I looked up and found Maya staring at me.

"It's okay."

"It is *not* 'okay.' Tell me the truth: Are you having difficulty swallowing?"

"Yes," I said, meeting her gaze. "But only a little."

"But it is too soon for that. You told me you had more time."

"I thought I did. But Captain Carcinoma has other plans, it seems. The tumor is more aggressive than we first thought."

Maya leaped to her feet and began pacing the lava.

"This bad! This is very bad!"

Was that real anguish in her voice?

"It doesn't really change things."

"Yes it does! Of course it does! You still have three more tines to claim. You will need all your strength to succeed. If you cannot eat . . ."

"I'll be all right," I told her. "I'll be fine."

With swift, almost jerky movements, she began packing up the food and closing the cooler.

"We have no time to waste."

She pulled a pair of long pants from her duffel and slipped them over her shorts. Then she produced the two pairs of gloves from yesterday and two machetes. She handed me a set of each, plus the flashlight.

"Follow me," she said, and we started into the brush.

5

I'd thought it was stifling before, but now we were way beyond that. We were following some sort of animal trail, using our machetes only when we had to, which thankfully wasn't all that often, winding our way through the thick greenery toward one of the black cinder cones. The air grew hotter and more sulfurous with every step.

We'd entered the borderlands of hell, where even the palmettos seemed to be melting. The trail had petered out a ways back—whatever animals used it were apparently smarter than humans and didn't come this far—but we didn't need it anymore, because as the ground became rockier and less hospitable, the trees and underbrush were petering out as well.

Finally we passed our last stunted palm and with only scrub grass to cushion our way we approached the scarred black flank of the cinder cone. Somewhere past the line where the grass browned out and died, we stopped at the bank of another kind of river: an obsidian channel of hardened lava.

This old lava had flowed and swirled around more permanent rocks that had been here first—granite, I thought—leaving them sitting like islands in the stream. The jutting stones among the lava gyres looked like a Zen rock garden done entirely in ebony.

"Didn't you tell me the lava was flowing?" I said, staring down at the rippled rock.

As if in answer, a jet of steam hissed through a finger-thick hole in the crust, about thirty feet to our right.

"It is flowing," Maya said. "Just below the crust, oozing from the heart of the cone to the lake shore. It has been quiet for many months. But now . . . that temblor last night must have disturbed it."

"How does that affect my getting to this fire tine?"

She pointed across the solidified flow. "They are over there."

Another steam jet let loose with a whistle.

"You're telling me I have to walk on a crust of old lava over a stream of red hot lava . . . just to get a tine?"

"Yes. The fire tines are on the far side, inside that crevasse in the wall over there. The best way to get across is to go from rock to rock, stepping on the crust as little as possible."

"Because it's so hot?"

Maya was staring straight ahead. "Because the crust could crack and collapse."

"You've got to be kidding, Maya. I'd have to be crazy to set foot out there."

She kept staring straight ahead. "Not crazy if it will help save your life."

Suddenly I wanted to shout at her that I had no proof that it would do one damn thing for me. All I had was new-age mumbo jumbo and her assurances. Not enough—not *nearly* enough!

But I said nothing. Instead I placed my gloved hand against my pocket and felt the shape of the earth tine through the fabric. I hadn't thought I'd be able to bring that one back, but I'd done it.

I studied the glistening black expanse, gauging the distance. Not much more than thirty feet across—forty, tops—to the narrow rocky ledge on the far side. Not far. And I wouldn't have to stay on the crust the whole distance—I could dash from rock to rock as Maya had suggested, making quick, short sprints that would keep my time on the crust to a minimum. But the zigzag course would take me longer, and I wanted to get this over with.

"Do I have to crawl through any tunnels this time?"

"No. The geode is embedded in the volcanic rock."

I knew if I was going to go at all, I had to go now.

"Here," I said, handing Maya the machete.

"What—?" she began, but before she could complete the question I was on my way.

I felt a sudden giddy recklessness perking through me. I had no idea where it came from, but a drunken stadium crowd that had seen too many Nike commercials was streaming into my head chanting *Do it! Do it! Do it!* and I saw myself scampering across the crust like a bead of water on a hot griddle.

I stepped off the edge with one foot and tested the crust with half my weight. It held, but God, it was hot here. One hell of a fire was heating this pan.

"Be careful," Maya said.

Slowly I increased the weight on the first foot, then brought the second down. A deep rumble reverberated through the crust and a mild tremor began to vibrate through the soles of my hiking boots. I was turning to make a quick retreat when the noise and the tremor stopped. I paused, waiting for more, but the crust remained silent. The noise reminded me of skating a frozen lake on a still morning, the eerie basso cracking noises deep in the ice that follow you as you glide along the surface.

But if you fell through ice, you had a chance of survival. No such chance here.

The memory of skating gave me an idea, though.

"Remember," Maya called from the shore behind me, "go from rock to rock."

Uh-uh. I was going straight across. And I had to get moving before my rubber soles melted.

I began sliding my feet, one after the other, across the crust. I had no delusions that I could glide across that pocked and rippled surface; the idea was to minimize the impact of my feet as I maneuvered my weight toward the far side.

It wasn't pretty but it worked like the proverbial charm—I was even considering patenting it as the Burleigh Lava-Crust Shuffle—until somewhere around the halfway point. I'd slid my right foot forward and was shifting my weight onto it when my boot sank with a soft *crunch*. I lurched to my left and snatched my foot free as a jet of steam and smoke, hotter than I'd have thought possible, hissed angrily into the air.

I heard Maya cry out in alarm. A series of booming *crack*s below the surface terrified me and I forgot about the Burleigh Shuffle. With my heart pounding in my throat, I scampered the rest of the way across like a frightened mouse with a hungry cat snapping at its tail.

I reached the far edge and leaped onto the rocky ledge. I crouched there, panting with relief. The surface was hot, but cool compared to the lava crust. To my left I could see the dark slit of the crevasse Maya had mentioned.

I looked back and saw her watching me from the other side, her hands over her mouth.

I straightened and gave her a jaunty wave, as if I did this every day.

"Made it!"

She lowered her hands and I saw her anxious frown. She pointed to the steaming spot were my foot had broken through. I looked closer and saw thick sludge, glowing a dull red, bubbling though the hole and oozing down the slope of the crust. As I watched I saw more pieces of crust breaking away, enlarging the hole, increasing the flow.

"Hurry!" Maya called. "The crust is beginning to break up!"

The old hindbrain was banging on my skull and shouting, *Screw the tine and get your irresponsible ass back to the other side!* But I was already across. If I could get my hands on a tine quickly, I was sure I could find a way back.

"Don't go away," I shouted—merrily, I hoped—then turned and ducked into the crevasse.

Sulfurous darkness, even hotter than outside on the crust, enveloped me as I rounded the first bend. The air burned my eyes, but at least the passage was high enough to allow me to walk upright. And I didn't have to worry about running into any dangerous creatures in this inhospitable cauldron.

I pulled out the flashlight and played the beam against the obsidian walls. They weren't smooth like the exterior surfaces. These were grooved and chipped. Hundreds of tools had been hard at work here long ago. I was stalking through a man-made passage. But what men had made it? And when? I passed crude carvings of big-breasted, fat-bellied women, obvious fertility symbols. The All-Mother?

But where were the tines? Maya had said they were right inside, embedded in the wall. Why didn't I—?

I cringed as pale red light flashed at me from directly ahead. My first fear was that lava had broken through the wall, and then I saw the geode—huge, even larger than the deposit with earth tines in the sand tunnel, but this one was exploding with pink crystals. And nestled in its heart, four tines of crimson-hued metal.

I stepped closer, momentarily taken by the glittering rosy fire. I allowed myself only a few heartbeats of wonder before reaching into its radiant heart and uprooting a tine.

I hurried back toward the light and stepped through the opening of the crevasse with my hand held high. But my cry of triumph never made it to my lips—Maya's stricken, agonized expression slowed it, and one look at the lava bed killed it.

A glowing, growing viscous river of liquid fire separated us.

Terror locked a fist around my throat as I realized what had happened. The little opening I'd punched through with my foot must have acted like a hole in a dike. The leaking lava had surged up, causing longer and deeper cracks, carrying away larger and larger chunks, until a whole downstream section of the crust had dissolved.

But I still had a chance. The crust upstream from my foot fault still held. But who knew for how long?

"Hurry!" Maya cried, telling me what I'd already guessed. "The whole bed is breaking up!"

If that happened, I'd be stuck on this ledge until the flow dried up and the lava cooled enough to form another crust that would bear my weight. That might be tomorrow, or it might be next month.

I shoved the new tine and the flashlight into my pockets as I moved upstream to my right. The ledge allowed me a scant fifteen feet before it merged with the mountain wall.

I stepped onto the crust and used the Burleigh Shuffle to glide the two yards to the nearest rock. As I leaned on the waist-high granite island to lessen my weight on the crust, I blessed Maya for bringing gloves.

The next rock was larger, lower, flatter, and fully a dozen feet away. I pushed off and shuffled toward it. Half way there I heard a *crack* like a rifle shot and felt the crust shift beneath me. Jettisoning caution I took two frantic leaping strides that would have put a Jesus Christ lizard to shame and landed on the next rock with both feet. As I teetered there, windmilling my arms for balance, a hair-singeing, eyeball-searing blast of heat swirled around me like a firestorm. I threw my arms across my face and bit back a cry of pain as the inferno seared the flesh of my forearms.

A scream from Maya echoed faintly behind more loud cracks. I lowered my arms and parted my eyelids just enough to see. I gasped searing air and struggled to keep my footing as my knees turned to melting rubber: upstream from me the crust had broken away in a huge "V." Thick, chunky molten lava now flowed lazily on all sides of my little island. Tongues of flame and puffs of acrid vapor reached for me from the glowing surface. Bursting lava bubbles splattered me with droplets of fire.

Terrified, I turned in a slow awkward circle. I couldn't jump back the twelve feet between me and the rock I'd left. And the next rock on the other side lay a little ways downstream and easily ten feet away. Another half a dozen feet beyond that, Maya's image wavered on the far shore like a mirage.

I was trapped.

I had never been so frightened or felt so helpless in my entire life. I had nowhere to go. I was stuck in the center of a lava flow that was slowly broiling me to a crisp.

I was a dead man.

I fought panic. There had to be something—

I started and turned at another loud *crack*. Looking upstream I saw a piece of crust break free and float by to my right. Then an even larger piece separated with a *crunch* and started to follow it. But this one migrated toward my left.

As I watched it approach, a desperate idea took shape in my head. When the chunk of crust came within a yard of my little island,

I jumped onto it. It tilted beneath my weight, almost pitching me backward. Dimly I heard Maya scream as I fought for balance. I had to keep moving, had to get off this volcanic flotsam before it passed the next rock. I dug the toes of my boots into the crust, took two stuttering steps across the wobbling surface, then leaped across the intervening lava.

My left boot landed on the edge of the rock island and slipped an inch. For a heart-stopping moment I thought I was going to fall, but then the ridges on the sole caught and I was across. I didn't pause. I kept moving, leaping off that rock onto the still-intact crust between it and where Maya stood. It crunched and crackled beneath my feet but held until my diving leap onto solid ground.

Pain blazed through my knees as I landed. I rolled and ended flat on my belly, scared, scalded, bruised, but alive.

Alive.

But I'd been so close to a brutal, agonizing—

I felt a spasm in my stomach, a surge of bile in my throat. I struggled to my hands and knees. My shaking limbs could barely support me as I retched. But nothing came up.

And then I felt Maya's hands on my shoulders, rubbing them.

"Oh, Will. Will, are you all right?"

I nodded, unable to speak right then. She tugged on my shoulders and pulled me to my feet. I wobbled on Silly Putty legs as she stared at me and I stared back. Tears glistened in her eyes.

She said, "I thought you were . . . were going to . . ."

I could only nod. My emotions were in an uproar. Truly, I'd thought I was going to be burned alive out there.

And then her arms were around me and mine around her and we were hugging each other and rocking back and forth. I felt Maya sobbing against me, and her gentle quakes filled me with wonder and light. And then I heard a strange choking noise, a lost, wrenching, pain-filled sound I'd never heard before.

I realized it was coming from me. I was doing something I hadn't done since I was a kid.

I was crying.

6

In pain and utterly drained, I was in no shape to continue our boat trip. Six months ago I probably could have handled it. But I wasn't that man anymore. Captain Carcinoma was draining my reserves.

We decided to spend the night on the lake. Maya seemed concerned about losing a day, something about so much to do before the full moon, but finally shrugged it off and said she'd find a way to make up for the lost time.

After I cooled and cleaned my burned skin in the water, we moved our gear from the lake shore to a spot near the lava flow. Yes, it was hotter, but we figured we'd be less likely to be visited by snakes and carnivores there.

I had no mirror, but I imagined I was quite a sight. All my exposed skin was bright red; I had second-degree burns on my arms and could feel some blisters on the right side of my face. My hair was singed all around and I'd lost both eyebrows.

"Before we do another thing," Maya said as we deposited the sleeping bags and the cooler in a little clearing, "we must treat those burns."

"I'll apply some of that bacitracin ointment," I told her.

"Your little tube is not enough," she said. "And I know something better."

While I removed my scorched boots, Maya disappeared into the brush with a machete. She returned shortly with a large root and some sort of cactus plant. I sat and watched her peel the former and strip the spiny hide from the latter, then mash the pulpy flesh of both into a thin paste in a bowl.

"This will help," she said, kneeling before me with the bowl in her hand.

I began smearing a thin coat onto my arms while she applied some to my face. I closed my eyes and luxuriated in her gentle touch. We'd broken awkwardly from our brief, tearful embrace there earlier, and quickly recomposed ourselves into our more formal roles. But now I was enjoying the intimacy of being her patient.

I had to admit to myself that I was becoming increasingly attracted to this strange, enigmatic woman. Was it merely the combined effect of the jungle, the isolation, the crises we'd shared? Or was it the woman herself? I leaned toward the former, because I could not think of another human being with whom I had less in common.

I was disappointed when she moved back and began tearing long fronds from a palm branch she'd brought back from her little trip.

"What now?"

She gave me one of her little smiles. "You'll see."

Abruptly I realized that my burns no longer hurt. The pain was flowing out of them like water through a sieve.

"My skin feels better already," I said. "I'm impressed. What is this stuff—an old Mayan recipe?"

"Even older. It is from the Olmecs. They are the people who preceded the Maya in Mesoamerica."

"So how come you don't call this 'Olmec country?'"

"Because they are gone and we remain. The Olmec civilization collapsed about 2500 years ago, and the Maya took up where they left off. Some of what I know and believe comes from the Olmecs, who anthropologists believe were the first civilization in Mesoamerica. But they are wrong. Far more of my knowledge has passed down from another people, a nameless race, the makers of the tines, who preceded them."

"The makers of the tines . . ." I pulled out the fire tine and ran my fingers over its hammered surface. "You mean this was fashioned and hidden away before Christ?"

She nodded. "Before Rome, before Cheops built his pyramid."

Wonder filled me. I looked up and saw that Maya had all the palm fronds stripped off. Now she began weaving them together.

"Were these nameless folk responsible for that carving on the wall near the fire tines?"

She shrugged. "Possibly. They are a mystery in many ways. The few anthropologists who know of their existence have had great difficulty proving anything about them. But I know they existed. Their blood runs in my veins."

"How can you know that?"

"I just . . . know. They were not builders like the Olmecs and Mayans. They worshipped the All-Mother and lived simply and in harmony with the world around them. They started the Long Count."

"What's that?"

"It is the count of days that has run unbroken for over five thousand years. Since August 11, 3114 B.C., to be exact."

"What was so special about that day?"

"Nothing that I know of. It is simply the day they began the count. They had to start sometime. The Olmecs continued the count after them, and the Mayas continued it after the Olmecs. We have a different number system than the rest of the world. You use base ten, we use base twenty."

I held up my hands and spread my fingers. "Base ten makes more sense, don't you think?"

"Why?" she said, pointing to her feet. "You have twenty digits, not ten. Our twenty-day *uinal* is the equivalent of your week or month— twenty days, not your silly seven-day weeks or variable-day months. Eighteen uinals is a *tun*, which is the only time we break from multiples of twenty—probably because 360 days is roughly the equivalent of a solar year. Otherwise, it is twenties all the way: twenty tuns is a *katun*; twenty katuns is a *baktun*. The thirteenth baktun, which runs about 394 of your years, will end December 21, 2012."

"What happens then?"

"We start the fourteenth, which will bring the Long Count past two million days."

As I watched her nimble fingers weaving the fronds into a circular shape, I tried to grasp the magnitude of counting millions of days . . . a count starting centuries before Cheops and his pyramid. The concept was staggering.

"Our view of time is linear rather than cyclical," she said. "Every other civilization ties its time to cycles of the moon and cycles of the sun, but both those cycles are unrelated, and neither runs an even number of days. A cycle of the moon is twenty-nine and a half days; but twelve moon cycles is only 354 days, well short of a solar year. And a solar year is 365 1/4 days, which necessitates your silly leap year. Here we ignore cycles and simply count the days."

I said, "Those mysterious first people, the ones who began the Count, sound pretty bright. Why aren't they still around?"

"They turned away from the Mother. They began to worship male gods who demanded wars of conquest and blood sacrifices. The same happened to the Olmecs when they turned from the Mother and began to worship their jaguar god. Both disappeared. We Mayas fell into the same trap. We built and built, we stripped the jungles and exhausted the soil—"

"Well," I said, "as far as blood sacrifices go, Mayas are pretty famous for their heart extractions, aren't they."

"That originated with the Nahua civilizations in the highlands to the north. My people's willingness to absorb and adapt to other cultures and beliefs is both a strength and a weakness. Unfortunately, we absorbed the wrong things from the Nahua. We adopted some of their gods, bloodthirsty male gods like the Aztecs' Quetzcoatl who demanded human sacrifices. We shattered our harmony with the Mother and soon after that, our civilization began to fail. We were already well into decline when the Spaniards arrived. If we had stayed in harmony with the Mother . . ." another one of her shrugs, ". . . the history of your so-called 'New World' might have turned out differently."

"So we're back to harmony," I said.

"Yes. Harmony. Always harmony. It is everything. Even the tines have harmony. Show me your new one."

I held up the fire tine and watched the light dance on its rosy surface.

"Isn't it beautiful?" Maya said. "Now bring out your earth tine."

I held the golden one next to the red tine and said, "I suppose this means I have two bed mates now."

"Yes. Keep both with you always. But before you put them away, clink them gently together, then hold them up to your ears."

I clinked, heard their tones, then held the red by my left ear, the gold by my right.

"Do you hear it?" she said, her eyes wide, hopeful.

"Hear what?"

"A blending of the two into a third tone."

I clinked them again and strained my ears, but all I heard were two separate tones—and discordant ones at that. Truly, I wanted to hear the third. I didn't want to dash the hope in Maya's eyes. But I wasn't going to lie to her.

I shook my head. "Nothing."

"Oh." Her disappointment was palpable. "But you will. Soon. At least I hope you will."

A huge, fat, black-and-yellow bee intruded on us then. It buzzed around my head—attracted by Maya's balm, perhaps—until we chased it off.

"See that bee?" she said. "We were speaking of harmony, and bees and flowers are a perfect example. Bees pollinate the flowers as they gather nectar for their hives. The pollination paves the way for more flowers to grow. More flowers means more nectar for the bees which leads to larger hives and more bees to pollinate the extra flowers. A cycle of creation without destruction."

"I gather it's a safe bet to say you're not a meat-eater."

"That is true. I do not eat meat. But I do not think it is wrong to eat meat. Anyone who has lived in the jungle knows that something is always dying so that something else may live. Plants die so that insects and herbivores may live and grow, so that they in turn may feed the carnivores. Life and death, eating and being eaten are all part of the cycle of earthly harmony."

"So why not eat meat?"

"I simply choose not to participate in that part of the cycle. As natural as it is, I no longer wish to be responsible for the death of another creature. We rule Gaea's surface. We have made ourselves masters of all that moves and grows; that mastery in turn makes us caretakers of all that moves and grows. And I do not feel we are handling that responsibility well."

I thought of the other Maya Quennell who'd been arrested at the logging camp protest in the seventies. I had a feeling that if this Maya had been old enough, she'd have been right beside her.

"You're talking about pollution, I take it."

"And the rest of the fallout from industrialization and technology run wild: strip mining, deforestation, soil erosion, acid rain, toxic dumping—you know the litany, I am sure. All of it hurts Gaea."

I wasn't going to let her off scot-free with that.

"But is your Gaea displeased with how technology and industrialization have improved billions of lives by offering affordable shelter and clothing and medicines and vaccines? Just look what's happened to human life spans. At the turn of the century, average life expectancy for the entire globe averaged fifty years. It now averages eighty. And despite droughts and famines, undeveloped countries have done even better—they've *doubled* their average life spans to seventy. And no thanks to Gaea—it's all due to human industry and ingenuity."

Her jade eyes stared at me a moment, then she sighed. "You have a point, I suppose. I simply wish we would stop and think and look for more harmonious means to reach the same ends. Is that too much to ask?"

"No," I said softly, and for an instant as I peered into her eyes I felt as if I were speaking to Gaea herself. "I don't think that's too much at all."

Her sudden girlish smile snapped me out of it. She held up the product of her leaf weaving.

"Here," she said. "For you."

I took it from her and stared at it, turning it over in my hands in amazement.

"A hat. I'll be damned."

"Perhaps, perhaps not, but you will most certainly be sunburned without it. We will be traveling in more open water tomorrow, and your scalded skin will be broiled before we reach our destination."

"The next tine?"

"Yes. The water tine."

"Water . . ." I liked the sound of that. Water I could handle.

We hunted up some bananas to go with the last of the beans and corn, and then I crashed. The predawn rising, the dugout trip, the fire ordeal all combined to leave me too tired even to boot up my laptop. I crawled into my sleeping bag and surrendered to the crushing fatigue.

But before it carried me away, I thought of Maya, how impressed I was with the efficacy of her homemade balm, how self-sufficient she was here in the jungle. From all I could see, the last thing she needed was money. So why did she want so much of mine?

With that unwelcome, unanswered question slithering through my skull, I dropped toward sleep like a rock off a cliff.

7

We were on the water again first thing in the morning, I in the front, Maya at the rear.

"Which way?" I said.

The hoarseness of my voice startled me. I'd been getting up hoarse the past few days, but it usually cleared after I'd been up a little while. Today it seemed to be getting worse.

"Your voice . . ." she said.

"It's just the volcanic fumes. Very irritating."

Maya gave me a look that said she didn't quite believe me. Frankly, I wasn't sure if I believed that myself. But I damn well hoped it was true. Otherwise it meant Captain Carcinoma was leaning on my laryngeal nerves.

She pointed toward the far end of the lake. "We head west."

The sun was setting a match to the sky behind us as we paddled across the lake's mirror.

I was feeling a bit shaky. Still the aftereffects from yesterday, I told myself. I put what energy I had behind my paddle, figuring I could work my way through the fatigue.

I was nearly bushed when we reached the western shore . . . which wasn't really a shore. This end of the lake emptied onto a slope of gentle rapids. The dugout scraped bottom as we poled it over the rim, and then we were moving fast, bumping and scraping against foam-framed rocks. We had a couple of bad moments, but then the slope leveled out and we slid into a stream much like the one that had brought us here.

I slumped back with relief as the current began to carry us along. A mix of willows and pines and palms crowded the banks on either side, but no signs of humanity. Too close to the volcanoes, most likely.

"Are you all right?" Maya said from behind me.

I swiveled and faced her as she steered. "I'm okay."

My voice was still hoarse. I found my water bottle and took a sip. It didn't help.

"I want to ask you something," I said.

"Perhaps you should save your voice."

I didn't want to save my voice. If Captain Carcinoma was to blame, resting it would do no good. I wanted to learn more about her while I still could talk.

"It's okay, really. I just want to know how much of this New Age stuff do you buy into?"

"I told you before: There is nothing at all 'new' about what I do."

"Okay. Sorry. You did say that, but it's the only way I know to refer to all the mumbo jumbo that's become so trendy in the last couple of decades. I mean, what do you think about, say, out-of-body experiences?"

"You mean spirit flight?"

"Whatever. Do you believe it's possible to leave your body and go floating around, looking at things?"

"I believe it might be possible."

"Then you've never experienced it?"

Her brow furrowed. "I am not sure. There have been a number of times when I thought I had left my body and wandered as a spirit."

"Really."

"But I might have been simply dreaming."

"What about flying saucers and visiting aliens."

"I have never seen any such things, but that does not mean they do not exist."

"What about those giant figures cut into the earth here in Mesoamerica, visible only from the air. Some people say they were directions for ancient astronauts. Do you believe that?"

"No. That is silly. If these 'ancient astronauts' could find this little planet across hundreds and thousands of light years, why would they need sign posts once they got here?"

"Exactly." At last—a purely rational response.

"Those figures were carved into the earth by peoples who had begun worshipping the violent male gods. They were not meant to direct visitors. They were meant to scar and disfigure the Mother."

The Mother . . . always the Mother. She was fixated on this Gaea thing.

"What about channeling? You know, when a long-dead person speaks to the living through a medium? Do you buy into that?"

"I have never channeled a discarnate, but I do not say it is impossible. What puzzles me is why someone would wish to take advice from such a being. Just because someone is dead does not mean they are wise. You could be channeling a very stupid discarnate."

I laughed. "Good point. But tell me, Maya—is there anything you *don't* believe in?"

She pinned me with her jaguar eyes. "Is there anything you *do?*"

"Of course. I believe in reality."

"Reality? So do I. Many realities, in fact."

"No-no." I shook my head. "There's only one reality: it's what trips you up when you walk around with your eyes closed. Beliefs that are contrary to reality can hurt you. No matter how fervently you believe you can levitate, the reality of gravity will deliver a succinct and decisive rebuttal when you step off the roof of a ten-story building."

"But that is physical reality. What about spiritual reality?"

"You mean the spirit plane, populated by ghosts and whatever? I've got one response to that: show me. Prove it."

"What about inner reality, then? You cannot deny that, Cecil. For most of us it is more important than objective reality."

"But it doesn't alter objective reality."

"It doesn't? Let us take a mundane example. Let us take a wealthy businessman who, despite all his successes, has never reached the impossible goals he set for himself. The world hails him as an inspiring success. He perceives himself as a miserable failure. Which is he, Cecil: a success or a failure?"

I didn't have an answer. Maybe because the question made me uncomfortable. I'd never been a businessman, but she almost could have been talking about me. Still, I didn't want to concede the point, so I hedged.

"Success is relative."

"So is science. Your scientific laws are not sacrosanct."

"No argument there. They aren't even 'laws,' really. They're theories that have been tested and retested under controlled conditions and seem to hold up under rigorous investigation. But that doesn't mean they're carved in stone. Scientific laws are being rewritten all the time as new information is discovered."

"So science is all theory with no facts?"

"I didn't say that. Look, Copernicus had a theory that the universe didn't revolve around the earth, but that the earth revolved on its own axis instead. It was called the Copernican Theory back in the 16th century, and he was damned for it. But since then the Copernican Theory has become what I think we can now safely call a fact: The earth is *not* the center of the universe and it *does* rotate on its axis. That's *reality*."

My already hoarse voice cracked on that last word.

She sighed. "Is that how your reality works, Cecil? From the way you talk it sounds like some sort of mechanical contraption rolling along an endless featureless plain toward a horizon it will never reach. My reality is a dense forest full of dazzling creatures and rich with mysteries and the promise of discovery. Which would you rather inhabit?"

I wasn't falling for that. My throat felt dry and thick, but I couldn't rest it yet. I sensed something important here, striking at the very heart of who I was. I forced my failing voice to challenge her.

"Reality is immune to my wishes. I want what is real, Maya. *Real*. I refuse to play the fool and buy into warm-fuzzy spiritualism because it makes me feel good, or because it offers the delusion of control

135

over chance and consequence. I need proof before I can trust. I can't be as accepting as you. It's not my nature. I've got to stick my fingers in the wounds—every time."

"Then you must change," she said gravely.

"How?"

She stared at me a long time . . . long enough to make me uncomfortable.

"You must find a way," she said finally. "I can point out the path, but you must walk it. Your science cannot save you now, so you must strike out on a tangent to your blindered *Weltanschauung*. Will you try?"

"I *am* trying."

"You must try harder. Open your third eye, Cecil. *See*—before it is too late."

I didn't know if I could. How do you strip away lifelong patterns of analysis? How do you adopt an approach to knowledge that is utterly alien to your psyche?

"Rest your voice," she said. "The current increases here. I will need your help to keep us straight."

The water picked up speed as the land began to slope. The stream widened as others joined it, and soon we were riding a small river meandering toward the lowlands in long, lazy switchbacks.

As the sun crawled higher and higher, I was glad for the hat Maya had made me. We began to pass small villages, then larger ones. Around midday we stopped at one of the largest we'd seen—maybe thirty huts. A toothless old woman in a tiny clapboard store with a corrugated metal roof offered us tamales in banana leaves, and a choice of warm Coke, warm Sol beer, or coconuts.

Maya and I both opted for Coke along with the tamale. I had a hell of a time swallowing the corn and vegetable filling, and had to wash it down with generous amounts of Coke.

But after a second Coke I perked up. Maybe all I'd needed was some caffeine. I hadn't had any coffee since my arrival in Mesoamerica. Maybe I'd been going through caffeine withdrawal.

Whatever the reason, I found myself with a lot more energy as we continued our trek down river. We ran into turbulent stretches but nothing I'd call rapids, and then the land and the river flattened out and we had to paddle again.

Where the hell are we? I wanted to ask, but knew it was wasted effort. "Maya Country" would be all I'd get. One thing I knew: all the mountains were behind us. We seemed to have descended to a vast plain.

The water widened into a broad swampy area filled with bushy trees that appeared to be perched on bowlegged octopuses.

"Mangroves," Maya explained.

The mangrove swamp slowed our progress. The twisting channels forced us to change course every few dozen feet, and kept us from building any momentum. But the slower pace gave us a chance to appreciate some of the fauna.

The mangrove trees teemed with life. Maya pointed out a spotted boa constrictor coiled on a branch, an occasional tree frog, but mostly birds. Purple-black crows hopped from branch to branch past large hook-billed birds, some with huge red breasts, that Maya identified as frigate birds.

We rounded a mass of roots and spotted a bird that looked like a red heron with a curved beak, standing in the water about thirty feet away.

"A scarlet ibis," Maya told me. "They were hunted almost to extinction for their feathers."

I took a closer look at the spidery mangrove roots and noticed barnacles growing on them.

"Are we near the ocean?" I asked.

"Very close. Less than an hour."

Maya was right, but it seemed longer. The mangroves trapped enough heat and water vapor under their branches to make a rain forest seem arid. But eventually they thinned. And now the westering sun was in our faces, but so was a cool briny breeze. I spotted low sand dunes ahead and we paddled for them. As soon as the dugout nosed into the beach, I jumped out and scrambled up the dune.

I stopped and stared at the sparkling azure blanket stretching to the horizon.

"Yes!" I shouted—or at least I tried to. Only a squeaky croak emerged.

I was amazed at the joyous thrill coursing through me as I began a little victory dance atop the dune.

"Surely you have seen an ocean before," Maya said, coming up behind me.

"Of course I have. But now I know where I am."

"And where is that?"

"On the Pacific Ocean."

"That certainly pinpoints your location," she said with a devilish little twist to her lips.

"Okay. Let me rephrase: I'm on the Pacific coast of Mesoamerica."

"And knowing that makes you feel better?"

"Yes. Absolutely."

"Then I am happy for you. When you are through celebrating, we must carry our things to a little village at the base of that cliff." She pointed north to a flat-topped rocky outcropping that jutted toward the sea like Diamond Head's little brother. A single tree grew tall upon the plateau. "We are spending the night there."

"Be right with you," I said.

I stared at the ocean a moment longer, reveling in the lapping of the waves, the tang of the breeze, and wondering why the sight of it made me feel so secure. Perhaps because I knew oceans and beaches, and felt I understood them. Perhaps because this was a particularly beautiful stretch of seaside, with an arc of bright white beach and tall broken islets jutting up here and there from the gently undulating water.

And the sand—buffed smooth by surf and wind.

Anxious to leave some footprints on that beach, I turned and hurried back to where Maya was unloading the dugout.

The seaside village of perhaps a hundred people was similar in appearance to the first village we'd visited, but more upbeat in spirit. The whitewash on the walls of the thatched huts seemed fresher, the colors of the people's clothing seemed more vibrant. Maybe it was because of all the welcoming smiles when they recognized Maya.

I spotted the Jeep parked under some palms, and seconds later Ambrosio appeared.

"You are burned, señor," he said, staring at my face as we shook hands.

"Could have been worse."

"But you got what you went for?"

I nodded. "Just barely."

"Bueno. Ambrosio is glad for you. Tomorrow will be much better when we go to *La Mano Hundiendo*."

I knew *Mano* meant hand . . . we were going to some sort of hand. "What's that?"

Maya said, "An island of sorts." She pointed northwest. "That group of big rocks out there."

About three-quarters of a mile offshore, a cluster of five cinnamon spires varying from fifty to a hundred feet high had punched up from the ocean floor. They huddled in a loose arc.

"What's it called again?

"La Mano Hundiendo . . . the Drowning Hand."

I looked again, and damn—with the tallest spire standing in the middle and the shortest and thickest sticking up on the near end, just like a thumb, it did look like the last desperate gesture of a drowning man, reaching for air.

The Drowning Hand.

Swell.

Dinner was rice and beans, with a little grilled chicken for Ambrosio and me. The three of us ate sitting around a fire outside one of the huts the villagers had lent us. I tried, but I couldn't get the chicken past my constricting throat. Only by mashing the beans and rice into a paste was I able to get anything into my stomach. So I drank lots of milk.

I excused myself from the fire and wandered down to the water. The sun had drowned but the sky was still alive with salmon and violet hues that surely had names. I just didn't know them. Venus was a brilliant point of fire, low over the horizon, rising in search of the moon.

I ran my fingers over the lumpy masses in my neck and worried. The Captain was running wild in there.

How long before I'd be restricted to a liquid diet? One day? Two? I'd be in real trouble then, because after that it wouldn't be too much longer before I'd be unable to handle even liquids.

And then it would be time to pull out the Kevorkian kit.

I had maybe a week to live. Most likely less.

The cold dark shock of that realization nearly knocked me to my knees.

Less than a week! And if I suffered a carotid blowout I could go in an instant at any time.

I felt so helpless and small standing there in the fading light. I hadn't wanted to die at home. I'd thought it would be much easier on all concerned—myself included—if I died where no one had to watch me, where I couldn't be hooked up to IVs and parenteral nutrients if I became delirious. And I was fairly sure I could arrange it with Maya and Ambrosio to deep six my Kevorkian kit after I'd used it so Annie and Kelly wouldn't have to deal with the fact that I'd picked the lock on the exit door and stepped through on my own.

The downside was I'd be dying among strangers, far away from home, and robbing Annie and Kelly of the closure they might need.

I kept asking myself: Am I being selfish? Am I only thinking of me?

But it's *my* life, dammit. Don't I have the right to choose where and how I end it?

I had no answers, and the questions were too burdensome to carry. I shook them off and returned to my hut—I'd have my own tonight. I focused on dealing with the more practical and mundane matter of sending e-mail to Kelly.

I lit up the computer and established a link on the first try. I smiled when I saw a "kellburl" return address; but something from Terziski also was waiting, and with an attached file no less. I downloaded both. Terziski's attachment—labeled "mug.jpg"—was a big one and took a while. After the download I checked the battery level. I'd used up only half its power; still a while to go before I had to pull out a spare.

I stayed online and read Kelly's letter. Her concern for my safety and health warmed me, so I pulled out her picture and kept glancing at it as I typed a reply. I told her about the lava, about the dugout trip to the Pacific, but said nothing of my purpose. I made it seem as if I were doing all these things merely for the sake of doing them. I told her I was fine. And then I came clean: I told her I missed her and I loved her, and that she was the best thing I'd ever done in my life.

All so true, and I wanted Kelly to know it, to have the words in black and white to keep.

A heaviness built in my chest as I typed. I didn't tell her that she'd never see me alive again, but I hoped this would let her know that I was thinking of her, right up to the end.

I uploaded the letter, then broke the link. I stared at her picture a moment longer before tucking it away. But the inner warmth fired by Kelly's letter vanished in the cold wind from Terziski's note.

Doc—

Something weird's going on with your psychic friend. Checked with the Oregon State Police on the Maya Quennell arrested at the logging camp protest in 1972. Just for the hell of it I sent over those latents I lifted from the business card you gave me. Believe it or not, they match.

Yeah. My sentiments exactly. What the hell's going on?

Your Maya Quennell is in her mid-thirties. I know because I saw her. Spent a whole day watching her. But according to the OR arrest sheet, so was this other Maya Quennell—age 34 back in 1972. That means she'd be in her sixties now. But we've got a thirty-something wandering around with her fingerprints. I know they can do wonders with plastic surgery these days, but hey, let's get real here.

The only explanation I can think of is that was her mother in OR and the old lady maybe handled the business card before our girl gave it to you. But then we should have three sets of prints on the card—yours, young Maya's, and old Maya's. I only found two.

And take a look at the attached mug shot. It's from the other Maya Quennell's arrest record. It's not too clear, being a scan of a Xerox of an old photo, but get back to me and let me know what you think. Must be a logical explanation, but I've got to tell you, we've got some majorly mysterious shit going down here, Doc, and it's starting to give me a case of the creeps.

—Terziski

Disturbed and puzzled, I opened the "mug.jpg" file and a black-and-white photo of a woman's face filled the screen. Terziski had been right about the quality—it was terrible. And yet . . . despite the graininess of the heightened contrast and the muddied half-tones, something eerily familiar seeped through and raised the fine hairs at the back of my neck.

A dark-skinned woman in her thirties with lank black hair cut in an almost boyish bob stared back at me with dark, dark eyes.

Except for those eyes, and the length of the hair, it was Maya.

Or her brown-eyed mother.

Or a much-older sister.

Someone with Maya's face and fingerprints, but not her eyes.

Fingerprints couldn't be changed, but a simple set of contacts can change eye color.

I grabbed the flashlight and brought it and the laptop out to the fire. I wasn't going to play any games. I dropped down next to Maya where she knelt and held up the flashlight.

"Do you mind if I check your eyes?"

She looked puzzled but not suspicious. "Why?"

"Can I? Only take about ten seconds."

"Very well."

"Just stare at the fire."

I leaned close and aimed the flash beam at her corneas from different angles. No sign of contacts. The jade color radiated from her irises.

I leaned back, not sure whether I was disappointed or relieved.

"Did you find what you were looking for?"

I held up the laptop and showed her the screen. "Who is this woman?"

I was watching her eyes. I know I saw her pupils dilate in shock. Her mouth compressed to a tight line as she shifted her gaze to me.

"Where did you get that?" she said.

"It was just sent to me. It's—"

"You have been investigating me?"

"Well, yes. I mean, I started to before I sold off everything and followed you here. Just as a precaution. I mean, wouldn't you if—?"

"That was then. When did you get this?"

"Tonight. I wasn't looking for it but, you see, the investigator I hired keeps finding—"

Her eyes flashed as she shot to her feet, but in her voice I heard as much dismay as anger.

"You are impossible!"

She started to walk away so I chased after her.

"Maya, you've got to explain this."

She said nothing, just kept walking toward the surf. I followed. I had to have an answer.

"Maya, there's a woman here from 1972 who's got your finger-prints and could be your twin except she'd be sixty-something now. I just want to know what's going on."

She whirled on me and jabbed a finger at my face. The fading light flashed off her bared teeth.

"I explain nothing! My *fingerprints?* It is *you* who must explain, and I do not care to listen!"

"Maya—"

"No! No more from you! You came here to learn to see. I told you how the past taints your vision and so you must cut yourself off from your material burdens and from your old life. You told me you brought your little contraption to keep a record, and to reassure your family of your safety, but you use it to pry into my life!"

Somehow this had gotten turned around. Why was *I* on the defensive?

"Listen—"

"No! *You* listen! You do not trust! The Mother wants you healed, wants me to guide you to the light, but I cannot do it if you do not trust me!" Her anger faded as hurt crept into her voice. "After what we have been through together in the past two days, how can you still mistrust me?"

The question was a knife in my heart. Suddenly I felt like a heel.

"It's not that. It's just . . ." I pointed lamely to the laptop. "I have so many questions . . ."

"Questions about the wrong things. Questions that I do not answer now."

"This picture . . ."

"Forget pictures, forget fingerprints. Do not look at me through your computer. Put all that aside and look at me through your heart, search for me with your spirit, force a ray of light into that blind eye—look at me that way and see if you do not trust me."

"I do trust you, but—"

"There can be no 'buts' to trust!" She turned and resumed her flight. "If there is no trust, then I can do no more for you and we will end your journey here."

"Maya, please!" I started after her again.

"Do not follow me. I have no more to say to you."

Maya was leaving me. Icy spicules of fear rattled through my veins as I watched her retreating figure fade into the twilight. I was losing her. And I realized in that instant how much I did trust her . . . deeply and truly. Yes, I had bothersome unanswered questions, but I had let them overrule the testimony of the time we'd spent together, all the hours and minutes that told me she was here on a mission, and the mission was me. Why had I allowed that? What the hell was wrong with me?

I tried to call after her retreating figure but my voice cracked and crumbled. "Maya! What can I do to convince you?"

A shadow among the shadows now, she didn't speak, didn't turn.

With desperation clawing at my back, I ran down to the surf line and hurled my laptop into the ocean.

"There!" I called, my voice little more than a harsh rasp. "It's gone! I've cut the last tether to the old me. I'm completely cut off now. It's just me here. Me and you."

I waited for a reply, or to see her emerge from the shadows.

"Maya?"

Where was she? I'd made my grand gesture. Wasn't that enough?

"*Maya!*"

But she was gone.

9

"Drink some of this," Ambrosio said.

I'd returned to the fire to wait for Maya, but the hours dragged on and she didn't show. I was vaguely aware of a nearly full moon drifting through the sky and lighting a path across the water, but I was feeling too miserable to appreciate it.

I'd blown this, but good.

Ambrosio had been chattering away and I'd been answering him with monosyllables, so when he'd upped and left, I figured he didn't see much point in hanging with me either. But he returned with an old wine bottle. He popped the crumbling cork and offered me a taste.

I held it out to the fire and peered through the unlabeled green glass. Half full, but the dark, cloudy liquid inside didn't look like any wine I'd ever seen.

"What is it?"

"A special mixture. Ambrosio make it himself."

Mayan moonshine, I thought. Okay. I could use a drink.

146

I took a swig, swallowed, and gagged.

"What *is* that?" I said after I stopped coughing. If I'd been hoarse before, I was really hoarse now.

Ambrosio took a swig of the foul-tasting stuff and passed the bottle back.

"Drink more. It will be good for you."

I was about to refuse, then figured, why not? Besides, the aftertaste wasn't so bad. Something familiar in the mixture. I took another pull, and this time I didn't cough.

"What's in this?"

"Rum, herbs, tobacco—"

"Tobacco rum?" That was the familiar flavor. I'd chewed some Red Man in college. "That's a first for me. What else?"

"And teonancatl."

"What's that mean?"

"'The flesh of God.'"

"No, really."

"It is true. Teonancatl are mushrooms that grew from drops of Quetzacoatl's blood that were spilled when thorns cut his feet as he walked the land."

An uneasy feeling stole over me. "Mushrooms? They're not the psychedelic kind, are they?"

"Sidekick . . . sidekick . . . ?" Ambrosio said, trying to pronounce the unfamiliar syllables. "I do not understand this word."

"They make you see things."

His eyes lit. "Yes! They open your third eye! Help you see! You have had teonancatl before?"

"No," I said, and handed the bottle back to him. "And it's a little late in life for me to start now."

He thrust the bottle at me. "No. You must have more. It will be good for you."

I waved him off, uneasy with the idea of psychedelic mushroom juice heading toward my nervous system. I'd smoked some pot in college—who hadn't?—but I'd never experienced anything even close to a hallucination. All it had done was make me mellow, horny, and hungry. I prayed that was all Ambrosio's mixture would do. Things were already quite weird enough here in Mesoamerica. The thought of being an uptight middle-class American freaking out in the middle of nowhere terrified me.

Filled with foreboding, I sat and watched the fire, waiting for something to happen. After about five minutes, everything still seemed normal, so I decided the safest course would be to go to bed.

As I was rising to my feet, the flames turned blue.

I locked my knees and blinked, but they remained a bright, shimmering Prussian blue.

Okay, I told myself. You're getting a hallucinogenic effect. It's just an alteration in color perspective. A spectrum shift. No biggie. Nothing to be afraid of. Just stay calm. The worst thing you can do is panic.

And then I heard a sound, a low, slow rhythmic beat from deep within the planet, like the pulse of an enormous heart.

The All-Mother? Gaea?

No. Just an auditory hallucination, the result of suggestion, a response to all Maya's talk about those Mother myths.

Then a higher sound, a keening tone, joined by another even higher note that blended and harmonized with the first. Then another, and another, higher and lower, uniting in a glorious resonance.

I saw Ambrosio beyond the fire. His lips were moving but I could not hear a word. He seemed to glow . . . a faint light shimmered and pulsed along the outline of his body.

And then a force took hold of my head and began pulling it around to the right. I resisted but it was too strong. I feared my neck might break if I didn't give in. So I turned and found myself facing the village, its surrounding jungle, and the looming plateau behind it.

Everything—the huts, the people moving about, the trees beyond, even the plateau itself—glowed with its own color, its own shimmering aura. And I saw other lights, soft, self-contained glowing forms that wandered unseen and unsuspected among the people and the houses. And there, atop the plateau, the solitary tree flared like a beacon, shooting a beam of light into space, up, up, up, as far as I could see.

Then my head was being pulled again. This time I did not resist, and turned until I was facing the sea, and I saw how it was alive with lights swimming above and below the surface.

I sensed the endless cycle of life going on about me, the pangs of births, the exuberance of growth, the fears and pains of death, the sour odor of decay as nutrients are given back to the cycle so that it may continue into eternity.

Then I felt the earth move. Not like the earthquake of a few nights ago, not a shifting of the ground. More a sense of . . . direction. I could feel the earth turning beneath my feet. Quite literally, I could sense the angular momentum of its rotational spin. I could also sense its headlong rush through space as it revolved around the sun, and its movement with the solar system as our galactic arm pinwheeled around the galactic hub. I sensed the pull of the monstrous black hole feeding deep within that hub, heard the flaring stars and planets cry out as they were sucked into its ravenous maw. And I even sensed the grander wheeling trajectory of our entire galaxy along with its sister star clusters as they fled ground zero of the Big Bang.

All moving . . .

Moving too fast!

I stumbled over to a glowing palm tree and wrapped my arms around it. The incalculable momentum, the titanic forces pulling at me! I didn't know if I was going to be pressed into the earth or flung into space.

I squeezed my eyes shut and cried out for help, but my own voice was lost in the wailing tones that filled my ears. So I just hung on, for dear life, because I knew if I let go I'd be flung into interstellar space.

And then after what seemed like hours of desperate clinging, I felt touches . . . gentle hands on me, caressing my shoulders, delicate fingers running over my face. Gradually the sounds faded, the terrible sense of motion slowed, and I heard a distant voice, calling from the far end of a long corridor. A woman's voice. Maya's.

I fixed on the sound, concentrated on it to the exclusion of everything else, and moved toward it.

"It is all right, Will . . . all right. You are safe and well here and I am with you. Nothing can happen to you while I am here. Do you hear me, Will? Do you?"

I moved closer and closer until I felt safe enough to open my eyes.

Dark. Night. My knees in cool sand. My face against a palm trunk. My arms around that trunk. And the world . . . stabilized.

"Maya?"

"I am here."

I dared to free one arm from the tree and find her hand. She squeezed it reassuringly.

"God, what happened?"

"Ambrosio did a very bad thing," she said, anger percolating beneath the words. "He gave you something he had no right to."

"Why would he do that?"

"He thought he was helping you, but this is not your path. You are not ready for teonancatl. You still have too many walls. You are not yet in harmony."

I finally released the tree and straightened up—cautiously. The universe seemed to have steadied around me, but the darkness had a strange hue. I faced Maya and saw a bright yellow aura around her, but it faded as soon as I tried to fix on it. I grabbed her other hand . . . to anchor me in case the planet threatened to hurl me into space again.

"You came back," I said.

She nodded. "Yes."

"I'm sorry if I offended you. I didn't mean to . . . I just . . . I can't seem to stop poking my fingers into the wounds."

She pointed her chin toward the sand near her left knee where a black square glistened wetly in the moonlight. My laptop.

"You did not have to do that," she said.

"You weren't listening. I had to show you."

Deep inside I still wanted answers, but I refused to let the questions get in the way. I was going to go with this, just let it happen. With a normal lifespan ahead of me, it might be different. But with the way things stood now, how much did a few questions really matter?

She said, "It is ruined, I am afraid."

Yes. Utterly. Sand and sea water were a lethal combination for microchips and disk drives. I'd cut myself off from Terziski and any further disquieting and distracting information about the various

Maya Quennells wandering the globe, but I realized with a pang that my impulsive gesture had also cut my line of communication with Kelly.

I managed a brave shrug. "Three days before the full moon, right? I gather that's the make-or-break point?"

She nodded gravely. "Yes."

Make or break . . . do or die . . . literally.

"I suppose I can do without it until then."

She rose and pulled me to my feet.

"You must sleep. Rest up for tomorrow when you must claim your water tine."

"Then you haven't given up on me."

At last, a smile—a small one, but a smile nonetheless. "No. You warned me you would be difficult . . . I just never realized *how* difficult. You are the challenge of my life, Wilbur Cecil Burleigh. And I will not be turned from saving you."

Did she really believe she could? Watching her, listening to her, I almost believed myself. Almost.

"Thank you, Maya."

"Sleep," she said, leaving me at the door to my hut. "We will go to La Mano Hundiendo at daybreak tomorrow, when the sea is most calm."

I stepped inside and almost tripped over the little table that sat just within the doorway. I bit back a scream when I saw a shrunken head sitting on its moonlit surface. I turned to run . . . then realized it was only a coconut.

I had to sleep this off. The sooner I got my eyes closed, the better.

I waited until my heart slowed to a normal rhythm, then felt around in the dark of the hut until I found the hammock. As I eased myself into it, the swinging motion gave me a bad moment—I thought Ambrosio's potion was taking hold of me again—but I held on and soon it steadied.

But inside, I was anything but steady. The hallucinations had shaken me, and still haunted me. I stared at the pale moonlit square of the doorway and hoped the rhythm of the waves and the insect Muzak would lullaby me to sleep.

I was just dozing off when a shadow crossed the doorway.

"Wake up!"

Someone stood silhouetted in the moonlight. It had a male voice and I'd have said it was a male figure, but the outline was strangely irregular.

"Ambrosio?"

"Captain wants to see you."

Not Ambrosio's voice. This was perfect English.

"Who?"

"The Captain, you fool! Get out here—on the double!"

Confused and a little dazed by the intrusion, I swung out of the hammock and stumbled to the door. The figure retreated as I approached, but when I stepped outside I wasn't in Mesoamerica anymore.

I was in a cavern of red stone, lit by . . . I couldn't find a light source—it was simply . . . lit. And the walls weren't really stone, they were soft and flexible. The floor sank a little under my feet, as if I were standing on a pillow.

My mouth went dry. Ambrosio's mushroom rum wasn't through with me yet. God, how was I going to get out of *this?*

"There you are!"

I turned and staggered back from the hideous figure looming over me. A vaguely humanoid mass of globular, blood-red tissue sat on some sort of throne where the hut had been. No mouth, no nose, just one huge eye in the center of its face. Blood oozed from its sloped shoulders where some sort of brass insignia had been pinned to its flesh . . . if you could call it flesh.

I stared in revulsion and it stared right back.

"You took your time getting here," it said. *"I wanted to meet you before it's too late."*

I didn't answer. What was the point? This was an hallucination. It had no mouth yet it was speaking to me. I wasn't actually hearing it—the words were taking form in my head.

But it seemed so *real.*

"What's the matter? You don't recognize me? Can't figure who I am? You named me."

And suddenly I knew—here, ripped from my subconscious by teonancatl juice, was the horror that had taken over my life, the one I'd anthropomorphized into . . .

"Captain Carcinoma."

"The one and only. Your worst nightmare, in the flesh. The new ruler of your kingdom." It raised a limb that vaguely resembled an arm. *"The King is dead! Long live the King!"*

I didn't know what to do. How do you handle a bad trip? Maya wasn't around to talk me down as she had before, so I was on my own. I vaguely remembered hearing something about how fighting it could make things worse, so I tried to play along.

"King of what?" I said.

It swept its arm toward the cavern behind me. *"Of all I survey."*

I turned and found that the cavern had changed to a Mayan village. As I watched, tumor people with globular flesh like the Captain but dressed in Mayan clothing were invading the village, killing the inhabitants and taking over their huts while Mayan warriors armed with bows and spears stood by and did nothing. The new inhabitants then began to remodel the seized huts into hideous, misshapen domes with no trace of symmetry. The once quaint, orderly community was being changed into a travesty. And still the Mayan guards did nothing. They patrolled the perimeter of the village, but let the tumor people pass in and out at will.

"See how easy it is?" Captain Carcinoma said. *"Your guards are helpless against my offspring. They are too terrified to try to stop them."*

Here in a Mayan microcosm was what was going on in my body: The Maya warriors were my immune system; they could have killed off the deadly tumor cells as soon as they appeared, but they've been programmed to fight *invaders*. Since the tumor consists of mutated cells from my own body, they don't see them as invaders.

"They're not terrified," I said. "They'd whip your ass if they recognized you as a threat. But since you come from me, they consider your cells brothers. They don't realize that their brothers are backstabbing psychos. Just like you."

"How dare you!"

"Well, what would you call self-immolation?" I said, turning to face the Captain. I'd been playing along with the hallucination, but now genuine anger was rising like the tide. Why not let him have it with both barrels? "You're an idiot."

The Captain laughed, an awful sound, booming yet strangled. *"Name-calling won't help you. You're doomed and you know it."*

"And you're not? You and your cells are useless. You're parasites. You do nothing but feed and grow and divide."

"And we divide so much faster than your cells. That is our strength. That is why our victory is assured. We are a new breed. A master race. We are over-running you. We will bury you!"

"And when you've choked off the channel that allows nutrients into the system, when your offspring finally seal off the tube that lets oxygen reach the bloodstream that feeds them, what will happen then?"

"You will die."

"And so will you, you goddamn cannibal!"

"Watch your tongue!"

"My tongue is where you were born! I'm your father. My cells gave birth to you. You're worse than a cannibal—you're a *patricidal* cannibal!"

Another booming, strangled laugh as the Captain shook its massive, cyclopean head. *"No, no, no! We call no one father! We birthed ourselves and we cannot die! We are different. We are supreme! We bring a new order, a new kind of life to your pathetic body. We will go on replacing your weak inferior cells with our own superior strain until every last trace of you is gone. Then our victory will be complete and we will rule."*

Captain Carcinoma was Hitler, Pol Pot, Saddam Hussein, and Osama bin Laden all rolled into one, riding a monomaniacal juggernaut to hell and dragging me with him.

I opened my mouth to try and explain, then snapped it shut.

What was I thinking? This was a mushroom dream, a creation of my neurotransmitters rushing through a psilocybin blender. Even if I could communicate with my tumor, I could no more talk it out of killing me than I could walk on the moon. Like all tumors, its cells had lost the Rb protein that controls cell division; it was a runaway train of ungoverned mitosis.

Had to get a grip. Had to end this now.

I sat down on the soft, sticky red floor and closed my eyes.

"Yes!" the Captain said. *"Kneel before your new master!"*

I covered my ears and began a tuneless humming to shut out its voice. One way or another I was going to take control of this. No more talking tumors, no more blood-red caverns and walking, talking metastases. I wanted the real world back, dammit, and I wanted it *now!*

I remained dimly aware of Captain Carcinoma raging around me but I steadfastly ignored it. Soon the sensation of the sticky floor faded from my bare feet and once again the netting of the hammock pressed against my back.

I opened my eyes. I was in the hut. Through the doorway the stars were fading. Somewhere in the village, a rooster crowed.

I sighed with relief.

Dawn.

10

"How does the world look this morning?" Maya said.

We sat outside her hut, eating a light breakfast of hard-boiled eggs as the sun struggled to clear the flat-topped mountain behind us. Maya wore her khaki walking shorts and a white T-shirt; the button protrusions of her nipples against the fabric told me she wasn't wearing a bra, and I tried not to stare. I wore a pair of Bermudas—the closest thing I had to a swimsuit.

I glanced around. Everything *looked* the same. The sea was a deeper blue than the flawless sky, the sand a creamy white—but scored now with an odd herringbone pattern that hadn't been here last night—and the palm trees lining the beach were their usual verdant hues. Everything was in its proper place, but somehow it all *felt* different.

A residue from last night's mushroom psychosis, I imagined. The world was the same, but I wasn't. I'd had some sort of transcendent experience, a glimpse into nature's creative processes, a feeling of oneness with the vast cycles of life and death swirling around me, of unity with the entire universe, and it had left me subtly changed.

Was this some sort of spiritual awakening, what Maya had meant by seeing with my blind eye? Or just a biochemical hangover?

"The world looks good," I told her. "Normal."

My belly rumbled like distant thunder and I realized I was hungry. I broke off some egg white, chewed it carefully, but it wouldn't go down. I turned and choked the pieces back into my hand.

"You cannot swallow anything?" Maya said, looking at me with worried eyes.

"Nothing solid," I said. "But liquids are okay."

At least they were for now.

I'd begun drinking a mixture of goat milk and coconut milk last night, but even that wasn't going down too easy. If we were near a town I could have bought some Ensure or another similar liquid supplement. But nothing like that existed around here, so this local mix would have to do.

I'd fastened my belt another hole tighter this morning. I'd been here only a few days and I must have lost ten pounds. I knew it wasn't just the change in diet and increased exercise: Captain Carcinoma and his crew were eating me alive.

"Are you well enough?" she said. "Strong enough to swim?"

"Not all the way out there," I said, gazing out to La Mano Hundiendo where the sun's rays where setting fire to the tips of the three tallest fingers. "Even on my best days—"

"We will take a boat to the Hand. But once there you must dive. Did you sleep well after I left you last night?"

"I slept, although I don't know if I'd call it 'well.'"

I explained my dream to her.

"You saw your tumor?" she said, her eyes alight.

"Well, yes . . . in my dream or hallucination or whatever it was."

"And you spoke to it?"

"I guess you could say that, but—"

"This is good," she said, smiling and nodding.

"Why?"

"You would not understand right now, but yes, this is very good."

She seemed heartened, and I was glad for that. The rift that had opened between us last night seemed to have closed, and I wanted it to remain closed.

I studied the herringbone pattern in the sand. It seemed to run off in all directions. I wondered if it was some sort of Mayan custom . . . go out each morning and use palm fronds to make patterns on the sand.

I was about to ask Maya about it when movement to my left caught my eye. Ambrosio and some of the village men were carrying a dinghy with a tiny outboard motor down to the water.

Maya rose to her feet. "Wait here. We will leave in a few minutes."

I watched as she walked off toward a larger hut where the village children were beginning to gather. Actually I watched her lean, muscular legs, the ropy pull of her hamstrings, the tidal swellings of her calves. Even in my weakened state the sight stirred me.

And then I spotted Ambrosio approaching from the beach. He wore a straw hat which he removed when he reached me. He avoided eye contact.

"Ambrosio is very sorry about last night, señor. He did not think—"

"Ambrosio," I said, rising and brushing the sand from my legs, "you don't have to apologize."

"Yes, Ambrosio must."

"Because Maya told you to?"

"No. Because Ambrosio did a foolish thing."

His humility made me uncomfortable. And truly, I wasn't angry. Yes, he *had* done a foolish thing, but I'd suffered no harm—I'd been scared half to death, but I'd survived the ordeal, and what was more, I'd had a new experience, something I'd remember the rest of my life . . . however long that might be.

I stuck out my hand. "Ambrosio, I know you were only trying to help, and I might even be somewhat better for the whole thing, so let's not mention it again. *Si?*"

He looked me in the eyes and flashed that big gilded grin when he saw that I meant it.

"*Si!*"

I looked over to where Maya was standing by the big hut, talking with another woman with the village children gathered around her. I watched her caressing the hair of the boys and girls who leaned against her, and wondered if she had any children of her own. Terziski hadn't mentioned—

No, I warned myself. Don't think about Terziski or photos or fingerprints. Just go with it.

"What is that?" I asked Ambrosio. "A school?"

"Yes. It is the sabia's."

"Maya's?"

"Yes. She built it. She pays for the teacher. She has built many schools for the Maya."

Without looking for it, I'd just found the answer to the question of why someone like Maya wanted my money. Not for herself, but for the children of her people.

As I watched her with the children, my throat tightened. Not from the tumor—from guilt. This was a good person, an extraordinary woman, and I'd taken so long to give her the benefit of the doubt.

Sometimes, Cecil, I thought, you disgust me.

"Come," Ambrosio said. "We go to the boat."

Maya joined us there and the three of us pushed the old wooden dinghy into the gentle surf, then hopped in. Ambrosio pull-started the coffee-grinder outboard, and we were off.

"Ambrosio tells me you built that school back there," I said as we left the shore behind.

"Did he now?" she said, giving me a sidelong look.

I held up my hands. "Oh, no. I wasn't quizzing him. Honest."

A tolerant smile as she nodded: "Yes. I built it. Education is the only way for the Maya to take charge of their future."

"Who's the teacher? A missionary?"

"Absolutely not!" she said, her eyes flashing. "The missionaries overrun Mesoamerica like cockroaches, but I will not allow them to teach our children. I will not have them tainted with Christian ideas."

I felt my hackles start to rise. I remember how the Presbyterian church of which I was nominally a member supported missionaries sent to Central America to educate the peasants. These were good people with good intentions.

"Tainted?" I said. "I can think of worse things than good works, love your neighbor, do unto others, and so on."

"So can I. But the missionaries teach the Christian view that the world is bad, a place of trials and tribulations that you must not allow to taint you. They worry so much about leaving the world that they forget about living in it."

"Yes, but is that a 'taint'?"

"Yes!" she said with fiery intensity. "Christianity and so many other religions warning of the supposed dangers and temptations of the earth, the Mother. They taint by teaching you to turn away from this world and set your sights on the next—turn your back on the Mother and see only the 'Father.' That is bad. That is evil. That is why, despite all their talk of good works and loving their neighbors and doing unto others, they still hate and kill each other, why they will go on hating and killing each other until they realize how completely wrong they have been."

How could I argue? Maya was an inhabitant of Mesoamerica, to which the Spanish had brought not only plague, but the Inquisition, and not a day went by without the news of the rest of the world confirming what she said.

"But let us speak of better things," she said. "Your water tine lies at the base of La Mano's thumb. You must dive for it."

"It's not in an underwater cave or anything like that, is it?"

"No. It's at the base of the rock, in plain view."

That was a relief. "How deep?"

"About thirty feet."

Thirty feet . . . I was PADI-certified in open water scuba diving. I'd been down to a hundred feet in Cozumel and Little Cayman and a number of Bahamian reefs during the past dozen years or so. Thirty feet with a tank was a piece of cake. But a free dive . . . ?

I looked around the dinghy for diving equipment and found nothing.

"No fins? No mask or snorkel?"

Maya shook her head. "No. You must enter the Mother's water as you were born, then let Her guide your hand to your water tine."

I started reviewing what I knew of free diving when something Maya had said struck me.

"As I was born? You don't mean in my birthday suit, do you?"

She nodded without a hint that she was putting me on. "Yes. As you were born . . . unless you were born with clothes."

If she only knew.

I tried to look cool about it, but the uptight-white part of my psyche—a not inconsiderable percentage of the whole—was going ballistic. I'd never been much for nudity, had never been comfortable with it. With Annie, sure, but never with my daughter. I'd never been crazy about locker rooms, either. That was how I was raised. If I ever saw my mother's breasts while I was nursing, I don't remember. Certainly I never saw them after I was weaned. Maybe my being an only child had something to do with it. But if you'd known my family, you might have thought we all bathed and slept fully clothed.

Don't get me wrong. I hadn't a thing against nudity—*other* people's nudity. As a primary care physician I'd seen more undraped human bodies than I cared to remember. And now that I was thinking about it, I refined my statement: I had nothing against *female* nudity. The unadorned female form is one of the visual wonders of the world. The male form, however . . .

Really . . . is there anything uglier than a scrotum?

But all that aside, the bottom line of the here and now was that I was going to have to get naked in front of Maya.

Remember, I told myself. You're the new Will Burleigh. If you could trip out like a hippie last night, you can skinny dip this morning.

As we approached the thumb of La Mano Hundiendo, I reviewed what I remembered about free diving. Every thirty-three feet of descent added one atmosphere of pressure to the lungs. At a depth of thirty feet I'd be subjected to two atmospheres—no big deal. But I'd read about something called shallow water blackout that happened to free divers who stayed down too long. The key was not to over hyperventilate before diving.

All right. I wouldn't hyperventilate more than the recommended three or four breaths. But could I get down to thirty feet and find the tine before running out of air? Piece of cake for an experienced free diver, but I was far from experienced.

Well, I'd just have to find a way, wouldn't I.

La Mano Hundiendo turned out to be much bigger than I'd originally thought. The spires of the fingers towered over us like the tops of undersea mountains. Close up, the craggy cinnamon walls looked like a bad stucco job. Swells surged relentlessly against the bases, spraying white against the flat surfaces and insinuating foam into the crevices . . . in and out, in and out, like sex.

Like sex? Where had that come from?

This was not the time to start thinking about sex. And yet, now that I was, I recognized an increasing attraction to Maya. But I couldn't let that progress. I knew I was vulnerable now, and if I let myself become infatuated with this shaman woman—infatuated, hell . . . I was sure I'd fall madly in love with her in a heartbeat if I let myself go—I'd no doubt make a complete ass of myself. She'd shown no sign of physical attraction toward me. Warmth, yes, but on a purely professional level.

Keep your head, Burleigh.

Just waves . . . Pacific swells . . . nothing sexual about waves . . .

The spires of La Mano Hundiendo weren't quite the naked rock they seemed from the shore. A fuzz of brush crowned their tops, accented here and there with scraggly trees and slim cacti gesturing defiantly with fifteen-to-twenty-foot fingers. And beyond those tops, screaming gulls wheeled on the morning breeze like vultures waiting for something to die.

Ambrosio cut the engine as we rounded the north side of the thumb, and I spotted a carving on one of the flat surfaces: another of the crude, big-breasted, fat-bellied women I'd seen near the fire tines.

"The water tines are directly below that carving," Maya said.

Thirty feet below . . .

I could do it. I had to do it. The hardest part might well be stripping off my clothes.

I hesitated, then said, "Oh, hell. Let's get this over with."

I pulled off my hat and T-shirt, then stood and turned away from Maya and Ambrosio as I unbuttoned my shorts. I removed them and the jockeys beneath together. Wondering what Maya was thinking as she watched my skinny, lily-white butt, I faced the carving and took four slow, deep breaths. Then I dove in head first.

The saltwater bit my healing burns and stung my eyes when I opened them and squinted into the depths. I immediately began stroking and kicking toward the bottom. The water was warm, blood warm, like the amniotic fluid of some giant womb.

I'd always loved the sea, had always been drawn to it. I'd been a water rat as a boy, one of those kids who'd go in and stay in until he was dragged out blue with cold. With scuba diving, no matter how large the group, I'd found a splendid isolation in the deeps: just me and the sea.

But now, naked, wet, and warm, I felt an even stronger bond. I was one with the sea. I felt as if I'd . . . come home.

I continued my descent, following the coral bedizened rock wall and waiting for a thermocline that never came—the water maintained its same blood-warm temperature all the way down. A rainbow of angelfish and clown fish made way for me. Popping, squeaking pressure built in my middle ears but I didn't want to break my stroke and risk wasting air to equalize them. I bore the steadily increasing pain. I wasn't going to be here long anyway.

The water was clear—not as clear as Cozumel's, but it had a good fifty feet of horizontal visibility. I spotted a wavering reflection below me. That had to be it.

My lungs started complaining then. I put more effort into my strokes and kicks, but I seemed to be swimming through molasses. Water plays tricks with light, and one of its favorites is making objects appear closer than they really are—just the opposite of the side-view mirror on your car.

I could see the underwater geode directly below, but my lungs were screaming for air now, the pressure driving ice picks into my ears, and I knew I wasn't going to make it the rest of the way. I turned and kicked toward the surface, aiming for the shadow of the dinghy and letting loose a stream of bubbles as I ascended.

When I broke the surface I clamped a hand on the boat's gunwale and clung there, gulping air.

Maya's face hovered over me, her expression hopeful.

I shook my head. "Found it," I gasped, "but couldn't reach it. Have to try again."

"Rest a moment first," she said, and reached down to give me a hand back into the boat.

"In a minute," I said.

I knew I'd have to get back into the boat. A surface dive wouldn't get me down to the tines—I needed the extra momentum of the leap from the boat. But I wasn't anxious to sit around nude as a jaybird up there while I caught my breath. Besides, the water was so warm and comfortable, I didn't care if I ever got out.

Finally, when I felt rested enough, I clambered up over the gunwale and immediately poised myself on the bow. I lined myself up with the carving, took four deep breaths, then plunged in again.

I had a better idea where I was going this time, and spotted the reflected light of the underwater geode soon after I opened my eyes. It beckoned from directly below. I stroked and kicked toward it with everything I had, but couldn't move as fast as I needed to. I was about ten feet from it when air hunger began hammering at my lungs again and I knew I wasn't going to make it. I forced another couple of kicks, got my outstretched hand to within about five feet of the geode, but couldn't go an inch farther. My air was gone.

Cursing my wimpy, inadequate lungs, I turned and kicked toward the surface with what little strength I had left. The need for air, the screaming urge to breathe was so strong I feared my mouth would open on its own and inhale water.

I was clawing upward, aiming for the dark wedge of the dinghy hovering above when another shadow intervened—about six feet long, blunt-snouted, swimming with a sinuous, almost serpentine motion. It moved off to my left as I rose past and I got a better look— slate gray body and black-tipped fins. I had a sense of it wheeling around to come back to me but I didn't pause to make sure. Sudden terror outstripped the air hunger already propelling me to the surface. I kicked like a madman. I had to get out of the water—now!

In a single motion I broke the surface, grabbed the gunwale, and scrambled over it without help. If the boat hadn't been right there I might have sprinted across the water to reach it. I tumbled onto the floorboards and crouched on my hands and knees, gasping hoarsely, not giving a damn that I was naked. Someone threw a blanket over me.

"What is wrong?" Maya said.

"Shark," I managed. "Big one."

Neither Ambrosio nor Maya spoke. Finally, when I'd caught my breath, I sat up and faced them with the blanket wrapped around me.

"Did you reach the tine?" Maya said.

"No. I got close but not close enough. I don't . . . I don't know if I can do it."

"You can do it, señor," Ambrosio said. "Ambrosio will teach you."

"That is a good idea," Maya said. "Ambrosio is an excellent diver. We will go into shore and he can give you some pointers while we wait for the shark to go away."

"Sounds good to me. But what makes you think it'll go away?"

"I have seen this shark before," she said. "He tends to come and go and he has never hurt anyone."

"You mean, not yet."

"He will be gone later. It is a Maya word, you know."

"Shark?"

"Yes. Only a few of our words have found their way into the languages of the world. That is one."

Maya fell silent. She frowned as she tugged on her braids and stared at the carving on the rock wall.

"What's wrong?" I said.

"So little time. You must obtain your water tine today, for tomorrow we travel to *El Silvato del Diablo* for your air tine."

"That means 'something of the Devil'—what?"

"The Devil's Whistle. And you must return with that tine in time for the full moon two nights from now."

"And if I don't?"

Her expression was grave. "Then all this will have been for nothing. You must bring all four tines to the holy place up there," she said, pointing to the plateau behind the village.

I followed her point to the flat-topped mountain with its single tree. "Holy place?"

"Yes. Tradition has it that a branch of the World Tree grows there."

"That tall skinny tree?"

"A ceiba tree. Some call it a silk-cotton tree, but my people call it *Yaxche,* the tree that holds up the world and the sky—the World Tree. They say the tree up there is a branch of the World Tree that has broken through from below. You must go there with your tines and place yourself between Gaea and the moon when she is full."

"That's a small window," I said.

She nodded. "The moon is Gaea's barren daughter. When she is full, she draws Gaea's power toward her, like the tide. The human body is mostly water—*salt* water. We all harbor a small sea within. The human body and its spirit have tides like the sea. When you place yourself between Gaea and her daughter at the proper time, the moon will draw her mother's power through you. Gaea will fill you . . . and change you." She looked away. "We will have only one chance."

I knew what she was saying, or rather, *not* saying: Barring a miracle, this coming full moon would be my last.

Ambrosio and I spent much of the rest of the morning and early afternoon practicing breath-holding in the shallows. He could stay under an amazingly long time. But as for technique, he wasn't telling me anything I didn't already know. Practice, practice, practice, sure, but a large part seemed to be natural ability, which I didn't have.

By late afternoon I was as good as I was going to get, so we hopped back into the dinghy and returned to La Mano Hundiendo.

I made three more dives, all unsuccessful. As a matter of fact, none of them brought me as close as this morning's second dive.

"I don't think it's a matter of breath," I told Maya as I sat panting in the boat. "I think it's strength. My muscles are too weak to take me deep enough before I run out of air."

"Can you try once more?"

I shook my head. "No use. Each successive dive is worse than the one before it."

Her crestfallen expression tempted me to change my mind, but then I glanced around and saw a gray, black-trimmed dorsal fin cut a winding path along the surface between us and the thumb.

"And besides, how could I concentrate on reaching the tines with him around?"

We all watched the shark until it wandered away.

Maya said, "Very well. We will postpone the water tine. Instead, we will leave early tomorrow for El Silvato del Diablo and return tomorrow night. You can practice your breathing while we travel and then we will try again for the water tine on the last day before the full moon."

"That sounds like a plan," I said.

"But not as good as my original plan. I wanted you to have at least a full day's rest before you climbed to the holy place. Now that will be impossible."

"Will I need all that rest?"

Her eyes locked on mine. "You will need every last ounce of your strength when you meet Gaea."

Meet Gaea . . . I didn't believe in Gaea, but that didn't stop a chill from dancing down my spine.

All that time in the water had exhausted me, so after a liquid dinner I was ready to turn in. But I had to speak to Maya first. I asked her to come to my hut where I opened my duffel bag and pulled out the Kevorkian kit.

I explained what it was for.

"Why do you tell me this?" she said, staring at the IV solution bags, KCl ampoules, and coiled tubing as if they were poisonous vermin.

"Because . . ." I wasn't sure how to say it, but I had to settle this. "Because I may need your help with it when the time comes."

"*When* the time comes?" she said. "That is your problem, Cecil. You do not believe, and because you do not believe, you have no hope."

She was right—oh, how right she was. And today had brought that home to me more clearly than ever.

Each new day meant more tumor. I accepted that. But where else besides my throat? Captain Carcinoma had its tentacles all through my body by now, eating me alive from the inside. That was why I was dropping pounds and losing inches. And more than just fat was disappearing. When cells—even tumor cells—shout for food, the body isn't particular about where it finds it. Fat cells are good storehouses of nutrients, but muscles cells also offer a rich supply. So I wasn't simply burning fat—I was losing muscle mass as well.

And that worried me the most.

"I'm wasting away, Maya. I've never been a terribly physical man, and I've spent my life in a sedentary profession. So no matter how much I practice breath holding—and I've got to admit Ambrosio has increased my hold time—I'm steadily losing the strength I need to propel me down to thirty feet. I'm losing this war, Maya, and you know it."

"I know no such thing." She looked away. "And even if I did, that doesn't mean I will help you kill yourself."

"Hopefully it will never come to that," I said. "But what if I hurt myself and can't insert the needle? That's all I'll need you to do—help me start the line flowing, and I'll take it from there."

"No." She rose and started toward the door. "I will not do that—I *cannot* do that."

"Then I'm out of here."

That got her. I didn't know if I truly meant it, but I had to make her believe I did. And I knew I had to talk tough to wring a deal from her.

She turned and stared at me. "You do not mean that."

"Absolutely. I have to know I can chose between a quick death and the lingering agony of dehydration and starvation. If you won't promise to be there for me when and if I should need you, then I'll go find a hotel room somewhere and wait for the end."

I wasn't bluffing, and she must have known that. She looked torn, uncertain. I decided to push her a little harder.

"You talk about my lack of belief and hope. What about you? If you really and truly believe I have a chance at a cure, why don't you simply say yes, you'll help me. What's to lose if it's a promise you'll never have to keep? That is, if you truly have belief . . . and hope."

I hated putting her on the spot like this, but I had to have the assurance of her help if I ever needed it. It was my security blanket.

"Very well," she said in a tight, flat voice. "You have my promise."
Then she turned and walked out.

I sat alone, feeling none too proud of myself. But this wasn't a game I had ever played before. I didn't know the rules, so I was making up my own as I went along.

The hut was stifling. The heat kept me from sleep, but it had help from a nagging guilt about backing Maya into a position she loathed, plus my worries about ever being able to reach the water tines. And then came all the regrets of my life—Annie, Kelly, roads not taken—recycling through my head for the thousandth time. I managed to turn them off . . . regrets were useful only when you had time to rectify them, and I didn't.

Desperate for some air, I crept outside to lay on the cooling sand and gazed at the night sky.

The moon wasn't up yet but Venus was low on the horizon, and so bright it cast a wavering bridge of light across the water like a miniature moon. I lifted my gaze and gasped when I saw the stars. They didn't have stars like this back in the U.S.—at least not in the Northeast. Where did they all come from? I hadn't seen the Milky Way since I was a boy, had almost forgotten what it looked like, but here it was now in all its speckled glory, a pale path of distant stars trailing overhead from horizon to horizon like a smear of semen from an infinitely fertile ejaculate, its countless spermatozoa streaming away into the night . . .

Semen? Ejaculate? I'd come up with another sexual image. Too long sitting naked in front of a woman with jade eyes and glorious thighs. I felt a long-lost heat growing in my groin as I fantasized a reversal of our roles in the boat today: I was the guide and she was the tine diver. I saw her clothes come off, watched her long lithe body poised to dive into the water—

I jumped as something pinched my leg. I sat up and saw a crab—a dozen, two dozen, a hundred crabs. The sand was alive with dark scuttling forms. Land crabs? Sand crabs? Fiddler crabs? Venus and the stars didn't provide enough light to tell and I wasn't hanging around until the moon rose to find out.

I jumped up and danced back to the hut, trying my damnedest not to step on them. For a moment I watched from the doorway as they scuttled back and forth across the sand in some sort of dance of their own. At least I knew the origin of the sand's morning herring-bone pattern.

I retreated to the safety of my hammock. The hut was still hot but it was better than risking getting nibbled to death by crabs.

11

We left early the next morning in the Jeep: Maya driving, I in the passenger seat, Ambrosio crouched in the rear among the gas cans and my duffel—I wasn't going anywhere without my Kevorkian kit. He had a lap full of giant palm leaves and he was stringing them together with some sort of vine.

"What're you up to, Ambrosio?" I said. My voice was even more hoarse and cracked than yesterday.

"This will help you reach the air tines," he said with a grin.

And that was all he would say.

I sipped slowly at my mixture of milks, trying not to wince with each swallow, and trying to keep it from sloshing all over the interior of the Jeep as we bumped up steep trails into the mountains.

We drove in silence, mostly. I was most hoarse—and swallowing was the hardest—first thing in the morning. The tumor tissue probably became edematous overnight, and only after I'd been up for awhile did it shrink some. I couldn't stand the rasp of my own voice, so I could imagine how it sounded to others.

And Maya seemed a little distant after last night's encounter.

Consequently neither of us was the best company this morning.

Eventually I noticed the terrain looking increasingly volcanic.

"Are we going back to the lake?" I asked.

Maya shook her head. "No. We visit a very old volcano today—or rather, what is left of it."

The terrain flattened into a high plateau. The vegetation thinned as the soil became harder and blacker. Finally the trail disappeared and we pulled to a stop at the base of a steep incline.

"We must walk from here," Maya said.

She handed me a coil of rope—the same we'd used in the sand pit—and shouldered her backpack.

"We're not going to do more spelunking are we?"

"No," she said as she started to climb. "Come. You will see."

We left Ambrosio behind, and he headed into the brush with his machete. As we climbed, I began to hear a strange sound, a mournful low-pitched hum, rising and falling. The farther we ascended, the louder it became until it seeped into my bones and buzzed in my head.

The ground suddenly flattened and we stepped out onto a high ridge overlooking an emerald sea of mountains and valleys. But directly in front of me lay a black hole. Not the astronomical kind—this was volcanic.

We were standing atop a volcanic cone. Its mouth stretched fifty yards across. The low moan I'd been hearing echoed from somewhere deep inside that mouth.

Maya moved to the edge but I held back. As I watched her kneel on the rim and stick her head over the abyss, I fought an urge to rush forward and yank her back. But as her head cleared the edge, I saw her braids lift and flutter above her head.

And then it all came together: the moaning sound, the wind pouring up from the depths—this was El Silvato del Diablo . . . the Devil's Whistle.

Maya turned and smiled. She motioned me closer. I got down and approached the edge on my hands and knees. The wind blasted my face and roared in my ears as I peeked over. I squinted against it and peered down smooth, sheer black walls dropping vertiginously to shadows of unguessed depth.

After a moment, Maya pulled me back. I didn't resist.

"The prevailing winds off the sea enter a wide cave mouth far below and funnel up through the chimney. During a storm it is quite frightening. The mountain's screams can be heard for miles."

I was only half-listening. I knew she'd said the so-called air tines were at El Silvato del Diablo.

"Where are they?"

She seemed to know what was on my mind. "The air tines?" She pointed directly across the chasm. "They're over there . . . around a bend to the left of that ledge."

I scanned the far wall, found the ledge, and made out a line of shadow where the volcanic wall seemed to fold around.

"Now how in the world do I get *there*? Crawl along the rim?"

"No. This is the only part of the rim that will support our weight. The rest is very thin and crumbly."

"Do we go around the far side and climb over?"

"No. The walls are very steep and smooth and hundreds of feet high."

"So what the hell am I supposed do—*fly* over?"

"Yes!" she said, smiling and nodding enthusiastically. "That is exactly what you must do! How do you know this?"

I thought she was putting me on until we returned to the Jeep and I learned what Ambrosio had been making with those palm leaves: wings. Even then, I wasn't completely convinced. I stared at the crude construction of leaves, branches, and vines and shook my head in disbelief.

"You don't really expect me to strap that on and jump over the edge, do you?"

"Si!" Ambrosio said. "I make these before. They fly plenty fine."

I turned to Maya, intending to say, You're joking, right? But then I realized that Maya didn't joke. Now I was truly perturbed.

"I can't do this."

"You must."

"It won't work."

"It has worked for others, it can work for you."

"You?" I said.

She nodded.

Here it was again: Maya had done it, so why couldn't I?

I felt shaky. Maybe it was from lack of solid food, maybe it was fear, or perhaps a combination of the two. I stepped over to the Jeep and swigged some of the milk mix, swallowing as fast as my throat would allow. After a few moments I began to feel better . . . less shaky, but far from relaxed.

I looked up and noticed Maya and Ambrosio watching me expectantly. I sighed. I'd already been almost buried alive in sand, almost roasted alive in molten lava, almost drowned. I supposed I could risk almost plummeting to my death . . . as long as we didn't forget the *almost* part.

"What the hell," I said as bravely as I could. "Let's give it a shot."

Ambrosio's response was a big grin. From Maya . . . a lingering look and a slow nod. What was she thinking? What was going on behind those jade eyes? Was all this necessary, or was she merely testing my limits, seeing how far she could push me before I'd dig in my heels and go no further?

I had to admit the wings were pretty ingenious—more like a kite, actually. Slim, flexible tree branches formed the frame, thickly layered palm leaves the skin, all bound together by tough green vines. Thicker vines strapped the frame to my body and formed handholds on the wings. The narrow V-shaped end of the kite was tethered to my left ankle; my right leg remained free.

"When you begin to fly," Ambrosio said as he tied the last knot, "hook your right foot over the left."

"When I begin to fly . . ." I said, grinning. "Now there's a prime example of positive thinking."

Where was the terror? For some reason, I wasn't nearly as afraid as I should have been. After the initial alarm, my self-preservation instincts seemed oddly muted this time. A side-effect of Captain Carcinoma's relentless assault, perhaps? Or were the rational parts of my brain overriding them? After all, if I went into a nose dive, what was the cost? I'd have advanced the inevitable by only a couple of days. A few dizzy seconds of tailspinning terror, and then instant, merciful oblivion, quicker than my Kevorkian kit.

I found an odd sort of peace in that.

Ambrosio started tying the rope around my waist.

"What's that for?"

"There are two dangers here," Maya said.

"You mean besides dropping like a stone?"

"Yes. The other is flying too high. If you get too far above the rim, the crosswind will push you out of the updraft—"

"And I'll go sailing down into the jungle."

She nodded. "Yes. We will try to prevent that with the rope."

"I'd appreciate that."

Ambrosio finished securing the rope, then checked all the fittings. Finally satisfied, he slapped my chest.

"You are ready to fly, señor."

I nodded and stepped up to the edge. I couldn't believe how cocky and reckless I felt. Looking across the windy chasm, it seemed damn near impossible for this flimsy contraption to carry me to that far ledge. But I didn't care. Was this how you felt when you've got nothing to lose? Whatever it was, it pumped me full with an exhilarating, untethered feeling: I'll try anything . . . the sky's the limit.

Was this how Icarus felt?

And I wondered how Maya had felt when she'd stepped off the edge with her own set of wings. She'd had everything to lose—but she'd had her beliefs to buoy her. I, on the other hand, was buoyed by the imminence of death.

I inched the toes of my boots over the edge and felt the moaning updraft whip my hair and tug at my face. I looked into the abyss, and damned if I didn't sense it looking into me.

Now I was afraid. And I knew if I stood here much longer I might change my mind. So I clenched my teeth, tightened my grip on the handholds, leaned forward, and leaped off the edge.

I screamed in terror at the initial seconds of freefall, then the vertical hurricane of the updraft caught my wings and I thought my arms would dislocate from my shoulders. But I held on. The descent slowed, then stopped as I wheeled in a wide slow circle.

Good lord, I was flying!

I began to laugh and shout and whoop, and might have sounded like some rodeo cowboy if I'd had a voice that worked. I was giddy, I was wild, I was crazy and goddammit I was really *flying!*

I couldn't see Maya and Ambrosio above me on the rim, but I could hear Ambrosio calling to me about my right leg, so I hooked my trailing right foot over my left ankle and tried to gain some control over my flight. I was gliding in a slow clockwise circle. I pulled down on my right handle, dipping my right wing. This brought me closer to the center where the updraft seemed stronger. I began to rise.

Now I could see Maya and Ambrosio on the rim—Ambrosio held onto the rope with one hand and waved with the other, but Maya seemed to have the fingers of both hands crammed into her mouth. I remembered what Ambrosio had said about the crosswinds and didn't allow myself to rise too high. I pulled down on my left wing handle and widened my gyre, moving outward toward the wall where the ledge waited. But as the wall raced toward me I realized almost too late that I'd pulled down too far. Just in time I let up on the left and pulled hard on the right and barely avoided splatting myself on the lava like a bug on a windshield.

I wheeled around again and gained altitude, then took it slow, easing myself toward the periphery. The ledge hove into view like a landing field. Luckily it was large enough to forgive the many errors in my ungainly approach. I unhooked my right foot and stuck it out, looking to make a one-point landing. I thought I was going to bring it off until my boot caught on a chunk of lava and I wound up skidding to a halt on my knees.

But I'd made it! I was here!

I stayed on my knees and sagged with relief. I let my pounding heart slow as I realized that I was nowhere near as cavalier as I'd seemed. I wanted to live more than I'd thought. That I'd just done something completely insane struck home with full force.

Finally I struggled to my feet and turned. I gave Maya and Ambrosio a thumbs up, then turned to the wall. I hobbled along the ledge, following it into a recess where I found another giant geode set into the rear wall. Four blue-hued tines nestled in its core. I plucked one free and put it in my pocket where it clinked against the other two. That was the easy part.

Now all I had to do was get back.

I found myself quaking at the thought. What had changed? I'd already done it. I knew now beyond a doubt that Ambrosio's wing-kite contraption worked, and that I could handle it. I'd done it once, I could do it again . . . couldn't I?

Not that I had a choice. Take another great leap or stay here and rot.

And then I noticed the wind-tossed rope trailing from my waist to Maya and Ambrosio on the other side. What if . . . ?

I visualized them tying their end to the Jeep, myself finding a place to secure my end over here, and then crossing the chasm hand over hand along the rope.

Who was I kidding? My failing muscles wouldn't carry me ten feet before giving out and sending me down the Devil's Whistle right into his gullet.

But I also knew if I stepped up to the edge and looked down again, I'd have one hell of a time taking that giant step. So I ran for the edge—ran as best I could with one leg tethered to the wing assembly—and took a flying leap into the void.

Again that initial sensation of freefall, and then being buoyed by the wind. I headed directly across. Circling seemed dangerous now, what with the possibility of slamming into the sides. The central updraft seemed stronger, or perhaps I hadn't been in the core of it before. It caught me full blast when I was halfway across and lifted me to rim level, then higher. I dipped a wing to take me out of the blast but I seemed to be caught. I was looking down on Maya and Ambrosio and saw them hauling on the rope, reeling me in. Yes. Do that. Reel me in like a kite. Get me back to solid ground. Now. *Please!*

It was working. They were pulling me out of the gale, and I was losing altitude—but losing too much altitude too fast. The rope was slack now and I was in a dive toward Maya and Ambrosio. I let out a hoarse, cracked, anguished cry of terror as I swooped toward them. I pulled madly on the handles in a clumsy attempt to flap my wings, trying anything to slow my descent.

Ambrosio leaped and somehow got hold of me. He did his best to break my fall, but as we both tumbled to the ground I landed half on him and half on a rocky protrusion. Pain lanced through my left chest wall as I heard the dull *crack* of a breaking rib.

Maya rushed over. "Are you all right?"

I couldn't speak. The fall had knocked the wind out of me and a knife stabbed my chest every time I tried to take a deep breath. Finally the spasms eased and I managed a few shallow breaths.

"No," I wheezed, clutching my side. "I'm not. I've got a broken rib."

"But you are alive," she said, kneeling beside me and taking my face between her hands. "That is what is most important. And you have your air tine. Now all you need is the water tine to complete your set."

I hated to kill the bright light of hope in Maya's eyes, but she'd find out sooner or later.

"You don't understand," I said. "If I couldn't hold enough air to reach the tines before, I'll never do it with a broken rib. It's over. I'm finished."

When I saw her crushed expression, I didn't know who I felt sorrier for: me or her.

12

An agonizing trip back to the coast. Every bump shot pain through my chest wall.

Night was falling when we reached the village. By the time we finished dinner—if sweetened milk from various plants and animals can be called dinner—the pain in my ribs had eased, but try as I might I could not draw a full breath.

Which meant my initial assessment had been on the money: the odds of my making a dive to thirty feet tomorrow had been slim without a broken rib; now they'd moved into the million-to-one neighborhood.

So I sat inside the door of my hut feeling miserable as I watched moonshadows migrate across the sand. Then a shadow stopped in my doorway.

Maya. She stood silhouetted in the moonlight. She wore a simple cotton shift and carried what looked like a large jar.

"I have something for you," she said, holding it up.

"Does it allow you to breathe underwater?"

"It is a healing unguent," she said, her voice soft as she came toward me. "An old Mayan formula."

"'Unguent.' There's a word you don't hear much these days. But no salve can heal a broken bone."

"One never knows. Take off your shirt and lie back on that blanket."

I did as I was told and she knelt beside me.

"Show me where it hurts."

I laid my hand across the bruised, tender swelling of my left sixth rib. "Right here."

Maya moved my hand away and began gently applying the unguent. It had a warm, creamy feel, slightly oily, redolent of rich soil and growing things. The inside of the hut began to smell like the jungle. Her fingers moved in slow circles, sliding over my ribs, leaving to dip into the jar, then returning to spread the unguent over a wider and wider area.

She hovered over me and brought her other hand into play. Now she was massaging my pectorals and shoulders, then my abdomen. Tiny electric shocks ran from her fingertips down to my groin. I felt myself becoming aroused.

"Turn over," she said, her voice husky.

I winced with the jab of pain from my rib as I rolled onto my belly, but it subsided quickly as her hands ran over my back, kneading the shrinking, wasting muscles and massaging the unguent into my skin.

When her fingers reached my belt line she whispered, "Loosen your belt."

More pain as I complied, but I didn't care. I was afloat, enveloped in a warm wet haze. Maya's hands slipped immediately under the waistband to massage my buttocks. Then she was tugging on the pants themselves. I lifted my hips to let her slide them off. And then I was naked and she was coating the backs of my thighs, behind my knees, then down to my ankles, an ancient priestess anointing a corpse for burial.

"Onto your back again," she said.

I hesitated—I was fully erect against the blanket beneath me—

but then I figured she had to be expecting that. So I turned over and felt myself become even harder as I jutted into the air.

Maya began working her way up from my shins, to my knees, up my thighs. Then her hands trailed away and I wanted to cry out, to beg her to touch me, please, just once. I didn't have to. She returned and gripped me with both unguent-laden hands, coating my aching erection.

I moaned, a low, almost pained sound bursting from the deepest part of me. I couldn't help it. It had been so long and her hands felt so good.

And then Maya was lifting her shift and straddling me. She was hot and wet inside, and I was greased like a Channel swimmer. I dove into her and began stroking, clutching the tops of her thighs and arching against her in a mad, frenzied rhythm while she held still, leaning on me with her hands on my upper arms. I was wildly out of control, completely at the mercy of the ecstatic pressure building in my groin and perineum. I erupted within her, my legs kicking and spasming as I released a hot, rapturous, pulsating stream that seemed to flow forever.

It took me a moment to catch my breath. I looked up at her, still astride me. She couldn't have gotten much out of that. Probably next to nothing.

Then she released a sigh, almost like a sob, and gently pounded her fists against the sand on either side of me—twice . . . three times.

I sensed her frustration. "I'm sorry. It's been so long since—"

"It is not that."

"Then what—?"

She pressed a finger against my lips. "Hush. Never mind. And it is not over yet."

Maya lifted her shift over her head and tossed it aside. She took my hands and placed them over her breasts. Then she began moving her hips. I was still inside her, but a lot smaller and flabbier than when I'd entered. The feel of her nipples hardening under my fingers, and the almost ceremonial way she was rotating and thrusting her hips began working their magic, however, and I was soon back to full tumescence.

And now it was Maya's turn. She leaned forward and gripped my shoulders, digging her nails into my flesh and moaning as she rode me. Finally she gasped and stiffened, rising and arching her back. I could hear her breath hissing through her teeth. As she made a high-pitched keening sound I thrust further into her and detonated for the second time. We hovered there, not quite on the ground, yet not fully off it, for I don't know how long before collapsing into a sweaty, panting tangle.

I took Maya's face between my hands and kissed her.

"You just fulfilled a condemned man's last request."

I kissed her again and tasted salt on her cheeks.

"You are not going to die," she whispered. "I will not allow it."

I wrapped my arms around her bare back and held her as tightly as I dared without jostling the splintered ends of my fractured rib. I felt rather than heard her sob, and I wanted to cry myself.

Oh, Maya, I thought. I wish you had the power to offer me a reprieve. Because now that I've found you, I don't want to leave you.

Never had I met a woman so antipodal to me and yet so like me. We seemed to disagree on everything, and yet never in my life could I remember feeling more sympatico with another human being, not even Annie.

The tumor itself was unfair, but to find a soulmate who could make life so worth living just when I was riding an express train to death's door was unbearably depressing.

I wanted to say more, but my eyelids were drifting closed, and suddenly I was dropping like a stone into sleep's ocean . . .

. . . dropping like a stone . . .

. . . seeing the stone hit the surface . . . watching a slow-motion splash, seeing the ripples spread as the stone sinks into the clear depths . . .

. . . sinks . . .

. . . like a stone . . .

13

Air hunger tore me from sleep.

Gasping and hacking, I levered to a sitting position, which should have sent a shock of pain through my chest wall but didn't. When the choking spasms eased, I touched the broken rib. Still tender but not nearly so much as last night. That unguent Maya had applied seemed to have worked. I'd have to find out what was in it and—

Listen to me, I thought. As if I'm ever going to have a chance to put it to use.

My throat was so swollen I could barely swallow my saliva.

I looked around and realized I was alone. I wanted her here, wanted to hold her, to tell her how curing me no longer mattered, that she'd transformed the remainder of my life. But Maya must have left during the night. I felt crushed. I hadn't heard her go. I'd slept like the dead.

But just before I'd dropped off I had an idea . . .

I struggled to my feet and stumbled to the door of my hut. I stared across the beach and the water to the spires of the La Mano Hundiendo. I thought I knew a way to reach the water tines.

But why on earth should I want to? I felt weak and sick, and I knew this was probably the last day I'd be able to swallow anything, so why devote my rapidly shrinking time and energy on such a fool's errand?

I couldn't explain it, but I felt driven to reach that last tine. Maybe it was because this was a task I'd begun and hadn't completed. Maybe I didn't want to leave behind any unfinished business. Maybe Captain Carcinoma was metastasizing through my brain and affecting my critical faculties. But as much as anything else, I wanted to do it for Maya.

I was determined to win my fourth tine before I died.

I spotted Maya standing with Ambrosio and my pulse quickened. Just looking at her gave me new strength. I realized then how completely I'd fallen under her spell.

I started toward them. Her warm smile when she saw me approaching made me lightheaded. I started to reach for her but a fleeting look of warning and a quick shake of her head warned me off. Why? Wasn't the sabia allowed a public display of affection? To have been with her, *within* her last night and now not to touch her . . . I might have been devastated if I hadn't sensed that her response would have been different in private.

"I want to try for the water tine again," I said in a dry rasp.

Maya looked at me with pain in her jade eyes. "But your rib, your strength . . ."

"I think I have a way," I said. "But I'll need Ambrosio's help."

"I do not know if this is right," Maya said as Ambrosio piloted us toward La Mano Hundiendo.

"How can it be wrong?" I said, straining to be heard over the little outboard. "I'll be entering the water as I was born, as you said I must."

"But you will be holding onto a stone."

"Yes. All stones belong to the Mother, right? I'll merely be taking one from the land and depositing it in the sea."

"I do not know," she said.

For the first time since we'd started this quest, Maya seemed unsure of what must be done and how to do it. And I felt like some sort of ersatz theologian, taking the premises of her mythology and interpreting them to my own advantage.

"It is just that I have never heard of it being done this way before."

"Well, either we try this, or give up. Because there's no other way I can do it."

Last night's image of a stone dropping into a pool of water had haunted me, reminding me of the weight belt that was an indispensable part of scuba gear. Why not use a heavy stone to speed me into the depths?

Before leaving shore, Ambrosio and I had scouted up a granite boulder that weighed in at a good fifty pounds. It sat beside me now in the front of the boat.

I watched the thumb spire almost hungrily as it loomed above us. I was in a fever now. The imperative to obtain my fourth tine had ballooned out of all sensible proportion. I was going to accomplish this, even if it was the last act of my life.

No longer inhibited about being naked before Maya, I stripped off my shirt and pants as soon as Ambrosio cut the engine. He came forward and helped me lift the boulder, then backed away when I had a good grip on it. My weakened legs trembled under the weight of the rock I clutched against my chest. Then I felt Maya's hands on my shoulders, felt her lips brush the back of my neck.

"Let the Mother guide your hand," she said.

I nodded and thought that Mama had damn well better guide my hand—I had only one boulder, only one shot at this. If I missed on this try, I'd have to call it quits.

I stared at the chubby fertility figure carved in the spire's flank and I took four breaths as deeply as the broken rib would allow, then I pushed the stone toward it and leaped off the boat. Keeping a deathgrip on the stone, I followed it into the water, letting it pull me into the depths. I kicked to boost our descent but almost let go when

I saw the shark directly below me. It darted out of my path and out of sight as I plummeted past.

I saw the geode approaching and released the stone as I came abreast of it. The granite continued dropping. My lungs were complaining as I reached for one of the green-hued tines among the crystals, but I still had air to spare. Why hadn't I thought of this before? I could have saved myself so much angst.

I snapped off the first tine I touched and kicked back toward the surface, my natural buoyancy drawing me upward. I glanced around for the shark but saw no trace of it.

As I had on every other try, I broke surface next to the boat, but this time I wasn't empty handed.

"Got it!" I croaked as I grabbed the gunwale.

I saw tears on Maya's smiling face as I immediately reached over and dropped the tine into the boat—the last thing I needed now was to drop it back into the water. As I heard it hit the floorboards, a feeling of peace swept through me. Mission accomplished: no more unfinished business.

But as Ambrosio was helping me into the boat I felt something sharp tear into my right leg, clamp on it like a vise, and jerk me back into the water. I gasped half a breath before I was dragged below the surface.

The shark! It could only be the shark!

I fluttered my arms in frantic, panicky strokes, fighting back to the surface, but it kept pulling me down. A strange mix of thoughts and images cascaded through my brain—I saw Annie in her wedding gown, Kelly in the newborn nursery, Maya leaning over me last night, and I thought, Is this how it all ends—eaten by a shark?

And then the terrible tearing pressure on my calf was gone, replaced by the sting of salt in an open wound. Dazed, numb, fighting shock, I clawed my way toward the surface, half expecting another attack.

Air! Where was the surface? How far down had the shark dragged me? I felt hands grab my arms before my head even broke the surface, and then Maya and Ambrosio were hauling me out of the water and into the boat.

Black spots were flashing and growing in my vision. I heard Maya's voice, high pitched with fear, saying "Oh no! Oh no!" I had a glimpse of my bloody leg before she wrapped a shirt—mine?—around it. A roaring grew in my ears, and from somewhere far away I heard Ambrosio.

"Lucky you so thin, señor. The shark he like the fat man. He spit out the skinny man."

I clutched at consciousness, desperately trying to hold onto it—I had so few moments left, I didn't want to waste a single one—but its hem slipped from my grasp and I dropped into darkness.

PART THREE

The Fifth Harmonic

1

Maya's voice draws me from the bottom of the sea. I struggle upward toward the sound, shivering from the cold of the depths.

Finally I pry open my gummy lids and see her face, that wonderful face with the jaguar eyes, shimmering above me. The image wavers and I let my lids drop, ready to sink back into the depths, but the voice hauls me up again like a fish on a gaff.

This time I keep my eyes open and look past Maya. I'm in the hut. Through the doorway I see a crimson sun sitting on the ocean.

Morning?

No. This is the west coast. That sun is setting . . . setting on my right leg, igniting it.

I open my mouth to speak but only a whistling gust of air escapes.

Maya shushes me and says, "Don't speak."

But I must. This time I form words, and my voice sounds like sand pouring on dry corn husks.

"The shark . . . my leg . . ."

"You have deep cuts," she says. "I have coated them with another unguent, and wrapped them. They will heal, but . . ."

"But what?"

"I will take you to a hospital if you wish."

"No!" Propelled by a vision of myself in a hospital bed, flattened between the sheets like a faded, desiccated plant in the pages of a scrapbook, I bolt upright and grab her arms. "No! Please!"

"But I don't know what else to do," she says.

"The Fifth Harmonic . . . isn't that why we came here?"

"But you are too weak. You cannot climb to the top of the hill."

She's right. I'm lightheaded just sitting up—the room is tilting and spinning around us, but I hang on. And I'm cold. In all this rabid Mesoamerican heat and humidity, I'm shivering.

I know what's wrong: the recurrent night sweats, plus a steadily diminishing fluid intake have left me severely dehydrated. My mouth is dry, and even if I had a normal amount of saliva I wouldn't be able to swallow it. My blood pressure must be in the basement.

Maybe if I go to a hospital . . . just long enough to get rehydrated . . . a couple of liters via IV . . .

Who am I kidding? Once they get their tubes into me they'll never let me go.

Tubes . . . IVs . . .

"My duffel," I say. "Get me my duffel."

Maya gives me a puzzled expression. "Why?"

"The Kevorkian kit."

Her jade eyes widen. "No, Will! It is not time yet."

"It will help me."

"No! I know I promised but—"

"Listen to me, Maya. I don't want the potassium now—just the fluid. The dextrose and water . . . directly into my circulation. It'll give me enough strength to—"

She smiles as her eyes light with understanding. "Of course! Of course!" She turns toward the duffel, then stops and turns back. "This is not a trick, I hope."

"No. Not a trick. I promise."

But if this doesn't work, I think it'll be time for the real thing.

I look down at the red-stained bandages on my throbbing right calf and feel the heat there. Ambrosio's words about the shark spitting out the skinny man drift back to me and I shudder. What if I'd been healthier and heavier? Perhaps Captain Carcinoma saved my life.

But if not for Captain Carcinoma I wouldn't have been in the water with the damn shark in the first place. I wouldn't even *be* in Mesoamerica.

And I wouldn't have met Maya . . . wonderful, wonderful Maya.

Trying to unravel that Gordian knot of chance and circumstance makes me even dizzier.

So strange how things work.

Reflected horizontal light from the sinking sun catches my eye and I see a rolled oilcloth. I uncoil it and there is my green tine. I hold it a moment, than arrange all four tines—red, gold, blue, and green—beside me, just like Maya's collection when I'd first seen them a world away in Katonah.

Maya returns with the kit and I remove one of the dextrose-and-water solution bags. Only 250ccs . . . I wish I'd brought the liter size. I unwrap the tubing and insert an end through the port at the bottom of the bag. I open the wheelcock and let enough run into the tube to chase out the air, but stop the flow before it spills—every drop is precious. I hand the whole assembly to Maya who holds the bag in one hand, the end of the tube in the other.

"Hang onto that for a minute and be ready to plug it in when I tell you."

Now I tie the tourniquet around my left biceps. I pump my fist to fill the veins. Considering the impoverishment of my body fat, I expect them to pop out like mole burrows in a barren lawn, but they barely rise . . . further evidence of my dehydrated state. I tap and slap at the antecubital veins to tease the blood into their lumens, and finally one begins to rise.

"There," I say, and reach for a butterfly—a short, high-gauge needle with plastic flaps attached to facilitate taping to the skin.

We have no alcohol, so I do without. My fingers tremble as I uncap the needle and press the beveled end against the flesh. I've got one vein here, and not a very good one. If I cause a blowout, I'll have to try the other arm, which means working with my left hand—not something I want to depend on.

I pump my fist a few more times, take a breath, then poke the needle tip through the skin. An instant's sting; I tighten inside as I see the vein begin to roll laterally; I push harder, chasing it, and am rewarded by a scarlet backflush into its short leader tube.

"Gotcha," I say to the vein.

I hold up the end of the leader and Maya plugs the IV tube into the receptacle. She raises the bag, I open the wheelcock to max, and the solution begins to flow. Since we don't have tape, I hold the needle in place as the solution bag deflates . . . slowly . . . the small bore of the butterfly restricts the flow, but at least it's flowing.

Maya remains standing and together we watch the bag like two couch potatoes before a television.

Finally the bag is flat.

"Squeeze it," I tell Maya, and she does.

After I milk the tubing, squeezing the last drop into my veins, I remove the needle and seal the hole with my thumb.

"How do you feel?" Maya says, watching me closely.

"Better."

No lie. I could do with a liter or two, but I'm amazed at the energizing effect of a mere eight ounces of sugar water infused directly into my circulation.

I glance through the doorway. The sun is gone, leaving only a bloody smear on sky and water to mark its passing.

"We'd better get moving," I say. "Take me to your leader."

"You must go alone," Maya says.

"Up that cliff?"

"The way is marked. I have brought you this far, but I can bring you no farther. What happens next is between you and the All-Mother."

I try to stand and I need Maya's help to get to my feet. A deep aching throb augments the burning in my right lower leg as I make a limping circle about the interior of the hut.

"How am I going to do this?"

"You must."

The thought of climbing to that plateau is daunting enough, but to tackle it without Maya . . . and then to face whatever it is I'm supposed to face, without my guide . . .

My heart starts to hammer in my chest. I don't want to be alone. Not now.

"Where will you be?"

"Down here, praying to the All-Mother that I have broken down enough of your walls to allow her power to enter you . . . and for you to recognize and accept that energy when it comes."

"But what do I do when I get up there?"

She begins to explain. . . .

The path *is* marked—if you call steps carved into the rock marked—but the climb is steep, and more often than not the whereabouts of the next step isn't obvious.

And the energy boost from the IV infusion is fading.

And my right leg is a molten lead weight.

I'm drenched with sweat, leaking the fluids I've so recently absorbed, filled with dread and yet strangely comfortable on this night so laden with expectation, no longer feeling apart from but a part of this place.

I see octets of spider eyes glinting from the shadows, I hear the sensuous rub of anaconda and poisonous fer-de-lance, the scurries and whispers of tiny night things, I sense the foliage around me coming alive and writhing to a primal rhythm beyond my auditory threshold, plucking at my clothing, inviting me to join their dance to the beat of the heart of the world.

Is all this the sum of my disease—fever, delirium, metastatic madness—or am I climbing into some sort of altered reality? I can't tell. Dehydration and its attendant electrolyte imbalances can do strange things to your brain, make you rammy, see things that aren't there, converse with people long dead.

I think I see Kelly sitting on one of the steps above me, but she disappears when I near. I see my parents, both dead now, frowning as they appraise the doomed, wounded, disheveled being their son has become.

They fade too, replaced by Terziski holding a picture of the brown-eyed Maya-faced woman. I don't stop. I climb right through him, I leave them all behind, hauling upward, ever upward like an old, old man with a ruined leg, using vines and branches as banisters to take the steps one at a time—raise the good leg, drag up the bad, raise the good . . .

Until the bad leg will no longer support itself and I must crawl, conquering each step on hands and knees.

Light floods from on high. I look up and see the full moon, Gaea's barren daughter as Maya calls her, cresting the hill, and never in my life has she been so clear, so intolerably bright, so frighteningly close that I can trace each mountain and crater on her sad, wounded face.

I'm late. I should be there now, on the plateau, arranging myself and my tines as Maya directed. If I miss the moon's zenith point . . .

Only twenty feet to go. I must double my efforts to reach the top on time, but I can't move. The tines are now leaden weights in my pockets. I have no reserves to call on. Aching with exhaustion and the heartbreaking sense of defeat, I look up and see someone standing on the steps above me, blocking my way.

You idiot, he says. *Look at you—risking life and limb to haul your sorry ass and a bunch of metal doodads up a hillside in the middle of nowhere. For what? For nothing. Because you know damn well that's what will happen up there—nothing!*

I stare at him and mouth the word, "Who?"

But he ignores my question and laughs.

A "Fifth Harmonic"? A "new level of consciousness"—give me a break, will you? Admit it, Willy boy. In your heart of hearts you know this is an empty exercise, the last act of a puerile symbolic rebellion against the science that failed you. So okay, you've made your point, and now it's time to cut the crap, get real, and find some modicum of comfort in what little time is left to you.

I recognize him now. The old me . . . fuller featured, better hydrated, better nourished. Was that what I was like? I hope not. The old Will doesn't seem to understand what's happened here in Mesoamerica. Maybe he's right that no new level of consciousness will be waiting for me up there. But that's not the point.

What is the point, then, Willie boy?

I'm not exactly sure. I have no double-blind, randomized, statistically significant answer to that. In other words, I don't *know* what will happen up there.

But I do know that I began this journey a week ago with a stranger named Maya. I know that this stranger has now become the center of my rapidly contracting universe. And I know that my journey will be concluded not with "some modicum of comfort," but atop this plateau.

Completing the journey I began with Maya—*that* is the end. If it proves to be a means to something else, wonderful—I am more than ready to be made whole again, to reach a new level of consciousness. But if nothing else happens, I will have no regrets. What I've seen and felt and learned on the path to this point is justification enough.

So, no matter what it takes, I will finish what I began.

And I know even the old Will must appreciate that.

"Get out of my way," I mouth, and he fades from sight.

Desperation fires my limbs. From somewhere in my wasted system I extract new strength and resume my crawl. The twenty vertical feet seem like twenty stories, but I don't look up. I look no farther than the next step. One step at a time, each its own Everest. Conquer one, and then the next, and the one after that . . .

And then there are no more steps. A flat, barren expanse of volcanic granite stretches before me. Toward the rear I see a tall tree with a slim, straight, branchless trunk, topped by a dome of leaves glowing silver in the moonlight. A ceiba tree, a silk-cotton tree . . . Maya's World Tree.

I'm here. On the plateau. I've made it.

I look over my shoulder at the world below, nearly day-bright under this brilliant moon. I see the roofs of the village, the white stripe of beach, and the glittering ocean beyond it. And on that beach, at the waterline, a lone tiny figure. Somehow I know it's Maya, standing there alone, watching . . . waiting.

I know she can't see me, but I wave. It's all I can do to lift my arm. Then I turn and start to drag myself across the rock. I try to recall Maya's instructions.

Not far from the edge is a large circle carved into the rock. You will find it in the shadow of the leaves of the World Tree.

With my eyes I follow the impossibly long line of the ceiba's trunk shadow across the rock to the splotch of black cast by its leaves.

Not far? Not for a walking man, perhaps. But a continent away for this crawling man.

I aim for the leaf shadow. The rough granite, still warm from the oven of the day, tears at my palms and forearms, and wears the knees of my pants. I struggle to within half a dozen feet of the shadow and stop, just about in. I listen to the harsh rattle of air struggling through my constricting throat and swear I've got no more to give . . . can't move another inch.

I collapse flat on my belly, panting, gulping sobbing breaths as I try to slide myself across the rock. I reach out, clawing ahead, certain that I can't advance another inch . . .

And feel my hand slide down a grooved wall. I lift my head. I'm there. A circular concavity, ten feet or so across, carved out of the living rock, stretches ahead of me. But only partly in shadow—more than half of its circular expanse is moonlit.

Maya's words rush back at me.

You must be positioned before the shadow of the World Tree flees the circle.

From the looks of things, that won't be long—I can almost see the shadow moving away. With a final desperate burst of strength I force myself ahead, roll down the six-inch edge, and crawl to the center of the depression. Along the way I find what feel like peg holes carved into the rock.

Two lines of holes cross at the center of the circle. They point to the four corners of the world. You must reach the center . . .

I do. I find where the lines cross, and slump there. Made it.

. . . and place a tine in a hole at each of the four corners. The fire tine must face the east . . .

I fish the tines out of my pockets and hold them up. The moonlight does strange things to them . . . the colors look odd, subtly altered. I glance around. I know where the Pacific is, so I insert the fire tine in a peg hole of the line heading the opposite way.

. . . the air tine faces north, the earth tine south, and the water tine west. Do not place them too far from the center. They must remain within easy reach.

Done, done, and done. I look and see the World Tree shadow hovering on the edge of the depression. Have to hurry.

Then you must lie naked on your back, touching the fire tine with your left hand, the air tine with your right, the earth and water tines with your feet.

I shrug off my clothes, stretch out on my back, and position myself according to Maya's instructions. I lay there under the moon and stars, spread eagled in the concavity like a plucked chicken in a skillet.

The moon is so bright it blots out the stars. And it's so silent here—the night sounds have faded away.

I turn my head and watch the last traces of the World Tree's shadow slide clear of the circle . . . and as it does, I feel a tingle in my right hand and see the air tine begin to glow.

Or is it just a trick of the moonlight?

I feel a similar tingle in my left hand and see the fire tine pulsing with a red light. I'm too weak to lift my head to check the other tines, but by the tingle in my feet I assume they're glowing as well.

And then I hear a sound . . . no, *sounds*. High-pitched notes, ringing softly in the night, just this side of my auditory threshold. It's the tines. They're ringing. I close my eyes to better focus on the sounds. I reach for them and find them, draw them closer. And as they near, they blend, harmonizing into a single glorious resonance. I open my eyes—

And cry out!

The moon has moved closer! It hovers over me, moving closer still, taking over the whole of the sky. I feel I could reach out and touch it if only I had the strength.

It draws closer still until I fear it will crush me. I feel the tug of its gravity, pulling me from the depression, but I grip the tines and hang on. And then I feel another force, this one pushing against my back, forcing my body upward until I'm stretched and bowed like some live insect pinned to a board. I can hold on no longer. The force from behind is ripping through my spine, erupting through my chest. I'm dying, I must be dying.

I scream into the vault of the night—

And then . . .

I am elsewhere.

I see nothing now, but have a sense of a huge void yawning around me, and I am falling through it. I feel as if I've left my body, and I wonder if this is death, if I am going to gaze from above at the empty shell of my body and then move off into that fabled tunnel of light.

But this lasts for only a heartbeat or two, then the void collapses and I am in a very crowded place, if I can call whatever this is a *place*, and I am still falling.

And now I realize that I am still in my body, truly *inside* my body, falling through it, completely aware of this organism that has housed me since conception.

Completely aware . . . not merely through the ordinary senses that filter through the conscious and subconscious, but in other ways that I never imagined possible.

Is this the new level of awareness Maya mentioned? Is this the Fifth Harmonic?

Whatever this is called, I am aware of every organ, every tissue, every cell in my body.

More than aware, I am *here*. I see the cells, I hear them, I feel them, and it's too much, too much, too much—the detail, the noise, the incessant activity, like being thrust into the center of an infinite hive of manic adrenalized bees, so much more than I can absorb or comprehend or tolerate. I must cut back the overwhelming input, shut down the feeds, and narrow my focus . . .

I constrict my awareness until I am outside a single cell. I press up against its soft translucent membrane like a street urchin outside a bakery window. I watch the raw nutrients around me slip through to the cytoplasm, I hear the rhythm of the organelles within as they assemble their assigned proteins and package them for export.

I too slip through the membrane, gliding past the mitochondria and endoplasmic reticulum toward the nucleus where I see the switchbacked coils of DNA arranged within, so close, so clear I can count the base pairs on the helixes.

I'm frightened. I don't understand this. What's happening to me? Am I losing my mind? Is this another hallucination, a late after-effect of Ambrosio's teonancatl juice?

But I seem to be in control here, and that eases my fears somewhat. I loosen the reins—just a little—on my awareness and gradually open myself to more cells and tissues. And as I do I become aware of a sound, growing in volume, ethereal, musical, yet distinctly unlike the tones I heard from the tines. These are sung by voices, tiny yet not high-pitched, hundreds, thousands, millions of voices, growing, swelling, not in my ears but in my consciousness. Myriad tiny voices, yet I feel I can pick out each one and hear its note.

And as I sift through the tones that make up this chorus, I pick out sounds of discord. Some only mildly off key, others harsh and atonal, grating voices that sour the harmony.

I isolate two discordant subchoruses echoing from opposite directions. I home in on one and flow there. As I near the source I sense increased activity, mounting steadily until I find myself in a war zone. My defense mechanisms are out in force: macrophages, the huge voracious cells that gobble up bacteria, viruses, and anything else they come across that doesn't belong, are rushing back and forth, attacking and digesting microbial invaders, protecting my repair mechanisms as they tend to the task of reconstructing landscapes of severely mangled tissue.

I realize I'm in my right calf where my cells are struggling to undo the damage done by the shark's teeth.

Struggling is the word. The defenders and the builders cannot work at full capacity. They're crying out to the rest of my body for the raw materials they need to manufacture the proteins for healing, reconstruction, and defense, but they're not receiving them. I search for a way to help, to increase the flow of nutrients to the war zone. I open the arterioles feeding the area; this increases the blood supply, but that's not the problem. The blood itself is depleted of nutrients. They're being siphoned off somewhere else.

And I know where.

I home in on the other discordant notes. These are louder, and originate at the other end of my body. I move toward the sound, aware of its source, dreading to face it, yet knowing I must.

In my throat I find the tumor. This is not the cartoonish Captain Carcinoma of my teonancatl dream. No lumpish megalomaniacal cyclops with a booming voice, this is the real thing—a megalopolis of cellular chaos where matted sheets of deformed cells with bizarre nuclei wail a mindless atonal cacophony as they grow, swell, divide . . .

grow, swell, divide in rapid cycles of mitotic madness—and it is so much more frightening than Captain Carcinoma.

Here it is . . . here is the mass of mutated cells that is slowly choking off my life. But where is the frenzied immune activity I'd seen in my leg? All activity here is the malignancy's. My defenders, my phagocytes and antibodies, hurry past, rushing no doubt to my injured leg, utterly oblivious to the monster that is devouring their world from under them.

Blind hatred explodes within me and I surrender to it. I yearn for a weapon so I can attack the tumor. I see a sudden flash of light and one of the tines—the fire tine—appears before me, alive with tongues of flame. The sight of it startles me. What am I supposed to do with it?

And then I know. I grab it and leap upon the tumor, tearing at the membranes of its cells, ripping them open, spilling their contents, rending cell after cell until I am awash in cytoplasm.

I stop, exhausted, surveying the carnage I have wrought . . . and it is negligible. I've barely scratched the surface.

I watch the surviving cells, the oblivious *masses* of remaining cells continue their mad, headlong race of division and multiplication as if nothing has happened.

A head-on assault obviously won't work. Nor can I replace the protective Rb and p53 proteins missing from each tumor cell. At one point, months ago perhaps, I could have made a preemptive strike when the malignancy was small and annihilated it. But now . . . now it is huge, its cells numbering in the billions, and it has colonized far-flung reaches of my body.

I am doomed unless I find a way to alert my immune system.

Desperate, I flow to one of the lymph nodes in my neck. Here is where the first skirmishes took place. The alarm should have gone out from here to the rest of my body—*Mutiny! Mutiny!*

But I see no signs of a struggle; instead an insidious fifth-column invasion has taken place. The tumor cells have quietly infiltrated the node and taken up residence, all the while continuing the wild division begun by their parent, and have crowded out most of the original occupants. Though the lymph node fairly bulges at its seams with malignant cells, the few remaining defender cells remain oblivious to them.

As I watch the tumor cells divide, I want to scream at my defenders to wake up and attack. Chew up the bastards and spit them out!

Maybe if I set an example. I still have the fire tine, so I thrust it into the chaotic nucleus of the nearest tumor cell just as it is preparing to divide. I use it to slash at the DNA . . . but the mitosis continues unabated.

I back away, defeated, discouraged. Frustration claws at me as the one cell becomes two. I stand helpless, crying out for a solution. What damn good is this new level of awareness, this vaunted Fifth Harmonic if I can't—?

Sudden movement catches my attention. A formerly idle white blood cell suddenly darts past me and leaps on one of the new tumor cells. It quickly engulfs it, then moves on to the other. I watch, stunned, as it devours the second.

What just happened?

I find another malignant cell preparing to divide and I use the tine again to slash at its nucleus. I watch closely this time as it divides and I notice a mark on the membranes of the new cells . . . an irregularly shaped scarlike defect.

And suddenly another white cell is there, engulfing the pair of new tumor cells.

It must be the scar . . . the defenders see the membrane defect as an alien attribute—a mark of Cain—and attack the cell as an outsider.

And now I see the other white cells stirring, alerted that something is up. Their membranes ripple as they scramble to readiness. They pause, then begin a frontal assault on the other tumor cells in the node—the *unmarked* cells. Some message has been passed . . . a marginally aberrant protein in the tumor membranes that previously has been allowed to pass is now designated as foreign.

The slaughter begins. The malignant cells have no defenses— they've survived this long only by their ability to pass as normal cells. Now that they've been unmasked, they're sitting ducks.

But even this is not enough. The tumor is too vast and widespread at this point. My immune system is weakened and disorganized, decimated by the months the cancer has had free rein to run wild through my body. Given enough time and a sufficient supply of nutrients, the system might be able to rebuild itself and conquer the tumor, but it has neither. Dehydration and malnutrition favor the greedy malignancy.

Demoralized and disheartened, I move away. If I could destroy the primary tumor mass, I could relieve the pressure against my esophagus. I could drink again. I could eat real food. I could build up my nutritional reserves and buy time for my defense forces. I could give this monster a run for its money.

But how?

I return to the primary site where the cancer was born. I stand on its border, in the teeming, burgeoning suburbs that constrict my esophagus and abut my trachea, and I glare at the blazing heart of its center city.

If only it had a true heart. Or a brain. A life center I could strike at and destroy. But a tumor is the soul of polycentrism—each individual cell is a potential new tumor.

I decide to travel to its malignant center anyway, to see where the end of my life began. The surest path there is along the tangle of new blood vessels the cancer has created to feed itself. I start to follow—

And then stop, my mind suddenly awhirl with possibilities.

New blood vessels . . . angiogenesis. A successful tumor has a knack for stimulating existing blood vessels to form new branches and send them its way to feed its growing cell population. A cancer can break all sorts of rules but it cannot get around the necessity of a steady blood supply to survive. No tissue, normal or malignant, can grow or even exist without that.

This one is no exception.

And here I am, watching my own pulsing arteries pump a continuous stream of blood into the tumor mass, feeding it. Can I do something about that? The tumor is already starving me—a little turnabout would be more than fair play.

But how? Find that tine and slash the arteries?

No . . . I want to kill the tumor, not me.

Block the arteries, maybe?

Again—how?

Can I narrow them? I can sure as hell try.

I start small. I concentrate on a nearby arteriole, willing the smooth muscle cells within its wall—*my* cells—to contract, constricting the lumen. And as I watch, I see a section of its tubular length shrink, reducing its inner diameter by a third, then a half, then all the way down to ninety percent. With only ten percent of the original flow moving through, the blood cells crowd against each other. I stimulate the sludging platelets to adhere, triggering a clot.

Done! The arteriole is plugged. Nothing flows through it now. Exaltation surges through me like electric fire.

The blood behind the blockage backs up to the nearest proximal branch and shunts away to down that channel. Keeping the first vessel constricted, I move to the next one, constricting and clotting its lumen exactly as I did the first. I keep moving, spreading my influence from vessel to vessel, tackling bigger and bigger arteries, systematically shutting down the tumor's life lines, cutting off its oxygen, strangling the filthy rotten bastard tissue.

The tumor begins screaming for more blood, for new vasculature to replace the suddenly defective infrastructure. But I allow no new vessels to form. I haven't been able to block every arteriole, but I'm throttling large areas of the mass, causing them to change color, turning them a mottled blue gray as those cells choke for oxygen. The tumor cannot move, but I can almost see it writhing in agony, and that only spurs me to clamp down harder on its blood supply. I scream like a madman.

Thought you had the playing field all to yourself, didn't you? Figured you had a lock on this, right? Well listen up, you slimy bastard! I want my life back. I'M in charge now, and you—you're fucking DEAD!!

The rational part of me knows that the tumor is not an entity, that it has no will, and can't hear me, but the rest of me that wants vengeance is in control now, and I'm Ulysses home from Troy, royally pissed and cleaning house. I'm wild, I'm crazed, I've been helpless so long before this monster that I'm out of control.

And then, at last, it begins. The tumor cells begin to lyse. That's a fancy scientific term for explosive cellular death. But I can't be objective here. If I had feet I'd dance. I watch with ecstatic glee as the membranes rupture and spew their contents into the intercellular spaces. Huge matted sheets of malignant cells leak and shrivel and die. The main body of the tumor begins to wither. And still I maintain my murderous stranglehold, clamping down until the bulk of its cells lie in ruin.

My own strength is waning, and finally I release control and let bloodflow resume to the area. White cells flood the region to begin mopping up the necrotic debris.

My vision blurs, the images waver. I see a flash and suddenly I am back on the plateau, bathed in sweat, lying on my side, coughing, retching, gagging. I spit foul-tasting tissue onto the stone. In the growing light it looks red . . . bloody. That couldn't be part of Captain Carcinoma, could it?

I look around. I'm still in the center of the circular depression, but the moon is gone, the stars are fading, and the sky is glowing toward the east.

What just happened? How long have I been here? I know I feel different, transformed, but I am even weaker than before.

My mouth fills with salty fluid. I swallow convulsively and—

Swallow? Did I just swallow?

"Will?"

I turn and see Maya hurrying across the plateau toward me. She's dressed in the long traditional huipil that covers her from neck to ankles, but even in the dim light she looks absolutely wonderful.

I try to sit up but I haven't the strength. I can't even speak.

She carries a container and as she drops to her knees beside me she holds it toward my lips.

"Can you?" she says in a voice thick with emotions—I hear hope and fear at war in those two words.

I open my mouth and she pours in a few drops of the milky mix that has sustained me these past few days. It tastes wonderful and I swallow it.

I swallow it!

I look up at her and nod. "More, please?"

And my voice, though still hoarse, is clearer—the pressure on my laryngeal nerve has eased!

Maya begins to sob as she pours more milk into my mouth. I can barely swallow it, not because of pain or constriction, but because I'm crying too. I get it down, though—I'm too ravenous and thirsty to let anything halt the flow of this marvelous nectar of the goddess—and between sobs she feeds me more, sip after sip until—

"That is enough for now," Maya says. "Too much will make you sick."

I nod. I want to upend the jug over my face but I know she's right.

"What happened?" I say.

"You tell me."

As I tell her about falling into my body, seeing my cells and manipulating my life processes, she begins nodding, then grinning, and her smile widens and widens until finally, when I tell her about strangling the major portion of my tumor at its primary site, she clutches my hands, throws back her head, and laughs.

"Yes! Oh, yes, Will!" she shouts with tears running down her cheeks. "You have done it. You have found the Fifth Harmonic!"

Had I? I'm not sure. Something wonderful and transforming has happened . . . something that finally deserves that misused, beaten-to-death word, *incredible*. But what?

"Is it the sound I heard inside of me?"

"No, no," she says. "The Fifth Harmonic is not a sound, it is a state of being, a state of complete harmony with your body and your self. It is the new level of awareness and consciousness I have been telling you about."

"But I thought they were just words," I say. "I never dreamed . . . I mean, I was conscious down to the cellular level. No, even further—to the molecular level."

"Not was—*are*."

"You mean, tonight wasn't just a one-shot deal?"

"Oh, no. Once you achieve the Fifth Harmonic, it is yours forever."

"I can go back in? Any time I want? Because that tumor's not finished, not by a long shot."

"Yes, any time you wish. You will have to go back again and again to root out all the metastases, but wait until you are stronger. You have no reserves right now."

Already I feel stronger. I sit up and experience a rush of vertigo, but the world stops spinning after a few seconds—the world, but not my brain. I close my eyes and try to sort through what has happened, try to make sense of it.

So easy to write off the night's experiences as a dream, that the only altered states of awareness and consciousness I've experienced are a very elaborate set of hallucinations. And yet . . .

I prod my throat with my fingers . . . the knotted masses of the lymph nodes are still there, but they're undeniably smaller.

And then there's the fact that I can swallow now, and my voice is coming back.

I can act like an idiot and say I'm still hallucinating, or I can simply . . .

Accept.

"But why did you have to be so mysterious all along?" I say. "Why didn't you tell me this was what I was after?"

She gives me a wry grin. "And how would Cecil have reacted?"

Good point. Excellent point. Cecil would have run screaming back to Westchester. Even now, parts of me are falling all over themselves trying to find scientific explanations for what has happened.

I catch sight of the tines, still sitting in their notches at the four corners of the world.

"The tines," I say, reaching out and clutching the fire tine, remembering how it placed the mark of Cain on a couple of the cancer cells. "They did it."

I see Maya shaking her head.

"What's wrong?"

"*You* did it," she says.

"What do you mean?"

She points to the tine lying cool and shiny in my palm.

"Dumbo feather," she says with a grin.

"You're not going to sit there and tell me that I've had this ability all along are you?"

She's nodding. "All along."

I gather up the other three tines. "Then why put me through the various hells of getting these things."

"You had the capacity but not the know-how. You did not know how to tap into your ability, and even if you somehow learned the route, you were too locked away behind too many walls to reach it. You first had to remove the blocks and strip away the layers of insulation that separated you from true harmony with your own body. Usually it takes years to find your way to the Fifth Harmonic, but you did not have those years, so I had to give you a crash course. And to make that work, you had to want to reach it badly enough to make the necessary leap to find it. The tines helped focus you, but the power was there from the start."

I think of Savanna and now I understand what she meant about "killing" her tumor. But . . .

"Wait a minute. What about Savanna? She didn't have years either. Don't tell me you hauled her down here and made her strap on a kite or play footsy with molten lava."

Maya's expression grows serious. "Savanna was open. Not closed like you. You had *so* many walls, Will. Even the other night, when we were together, when you were inside me, I tried to reach inside you. I thought your walls might drop then, but they did not. Even at the height of passion, they kept me from you."

That explains the way she pounded her fists against the sand. So it wasn't purely sexual frustration.

"Savanna was relatively easy," Maya says. "She did not have your walls. Nor did she have your level of ability."

"I don't get it."

"Haven't you realized yet that you are special? That you are a curandero?"

"A healer."

"Yes. Like me. There are not many of us. That is why the Mother wanted you saved."

"Then not everybody can do what I just did?"

"We all have a self-healing power, but to varying degrees—some have very little, some have more. Savanna has an average level, but she couldn't have cured herself. Her tumor was too strong. She needed help."

"Which you gave her."

"Yes. Every so often someone comes along who not only can cure the self, but can guide others to a cure as well."

I reach for the container and sip more of the milk mix as I try to fathom what Maya is saying.

"And I am one of those."

Her eyes fairly glow. "Yes. You were born to heal. It is a fire within you. That is why you went against your father's wishes and chose medicine over law. That is why your personal life suffered because of your practice, why medicine always seemed to be the most important thing in your life. You are a healer, Will. It is as much a part of you as your fingerprints and the color of your skin. And now you can go on healing, but in a new and different way, a better way."

"How? By entering a body and adjusting its physiology like I just did to myself?"

The residual Old Will tries to reject this, but I hammer him down.

Accept . . . accept . . .

Maya is nodding. "If the patient will let you. You cannot enter someone who does not want you. They must accept you."

"That's . . . that's frightening."

"Yes. Yes, it is. It is terrifying at first. And not always successful. Sometimes they will let you in but their systems will resist you. But when you and the patient are in harmony, you can work cures that seem miraculous. It is an indescribably glorious feeling, Will."

Wonder fills me as I consider the implications. A vast vista of healing stretches before me. The power to restore bodies and change lives for the better, to give people a second chance like the one I've just received . . .

And suddenly I'm depressed.

"All these years," I say. "What I could have done if I'd only known. I've wasted so much time. I wish you'd found me sooner."

"So do I," she says softly, staring at me. "For many reasons."

I take her hand. "Yes. Why did I have to wait till middle age to find you . . . to find myself? We've got no time to waste, Maya." My mind is filling, overflowing with possibilities. "We can do more than cure one person at a time. We can use our abilities to advance the entire field of medicine. We can *see* the workings of cells, sick and well. Imagine what a research tool this power can be! We can trigger a golden age of medicine!"

She's shaking her head. "Time is not a problem. But advancing the field of medicine . . . that is quite a problem."

"Why? When they see—"

"But they will not see. The field of medicine, the entire world of science is filled with people like Wilbur Cecil Burleigh. You remember him, don't you?"

The truth of that is a bucket of cold water on the flame that was sputtering to life within me. I remember the man I was a week ago. I can imagine someone coming to him and saying, *I have consciousness down to the cellular level.*

Yeah, sure, buddy. And I've got a flying saucer parked outside that'll take you back to Alpha Centauri.

But I'm not giving up.

"I'll find a way. But it'll take time and we've none to waste."

"Don't worry about time," she says. "You will have as much as you want. But before you go anywhere or do anything you must get to know your power, learn its limits, become comfortable with it, explore every nook and cranny of your body. You must chase down and eliminate the cancer cells to the very last one. Then you must search out other trouble spots in your body, and learn to repair them: find the narrowing arteries and clear them, restore worn cartilage in arthritic joints, replace aging or damaged cells with new ones—"

Wonder fills me. "I can do that?"

"Of course. You are in complete control of your body now."

"But if I can replace aging cells . . ."

"Yes?" Her voice is heavy with expectation.

"Then I don't have to . . ."

A slow smile is stretching her lips, deepening her dimples. "Did I not tell you that time is not a problem?"

And now all my slowly growing strength seems to desert me in a rush. I have to put out a hand to keep from falling back onto the stone. The nagging questions, the contradictions about the various Maya Quennells in Terziski's reports tumble back to me.

"Maya," I say, and my voice is hoarse again, but not from the tumor. "The Maya Quennell who graduated from the Sorbonne in 1938 . . . who is she?"

"Me."

"And the Maya Quennell arrested at the Oregon logging camp in 1972?"

"Also me. I could not sit idly by and let them cut down the Mother's wonderful ancient trees to make wood pulp."

Overwhelmed, I close my eyes. "Maya . . . how old are you?"

"I will be ninety next March."

She says it so casually.

"But your eyes . . . they're different from the eyes in the mug shot. Did you . . .?"

"Change them? Yes. When I was arrested and booked, I realized that I was leaving behind a photographic record that might catch up to me later. I thought changing my eye color from dark brown to light green would be enough. I know now that I should have changed my fingerprints as well."

"You can do that?"

"*We* can do that. It takes much time and patience, but many changes are possible."

"But why do you want to keep your power a secret?"

Her lips settled into a tight, grim line. "Do you think you can present your power to the world and be welcomed with open arms? You will learn that the world is filled with individuals and organizations—especially the scientific communities and the world-hating religions—who will see you as a threat. We must tread softly, Will. We must do our work in the interstices and always be on the lookout for others like us."

I know she is right about the threat we present to certain powerful segments of the world, yet I am not sure that I can keep this new power hidden forever. Maya is wise and she's been at this so much longer. I will follow her lead . . . for now.

She seems to read my mind.

"Do not think you can go back to who you were, what you were, and where you were. If you try, you will regret it."

Maya rises and holds out her hands to me. I take them and let her pull me to my feet. My muscles are weak and my shaky legs threaten to buckle, but I struggle upright and lock my knees as she wraps me in her arms and whispers in my ear.

"Your new life does not come without a price, Will. The old you is gone. You have emerged from the chrysalis that was Wilbur Cecil Burleigh. A line has been drawn across the course of your life, and you can never cross back. From this moment onward you will see the world—life, existence, *everything*—in a new light that will keep you one step removed from most of humanity. You will be different, Will, and people will sense that."

"What do I care about other people if I have you?" I say. "Because

I truly love you, Maya." And I've never meant that as much as I do now. This is more than a beautiful, loving, caring woman, this is a soulmate. If there is a Sixth Harmonic, it is what I feel when I look at Maya. All other women—all other *people*—I have known in my life seem to have lost substance, faded, dissipated, until there is only Maya. "I loved you yesterday morning, and I love you now, and I will love you as long as I breathe."

I hear her sob. I try to push back to see her face but she clings to me. "What's wrong?"

"I have been so lonely."

And I realize how isolated she must have been all these years. Never aging while everyone she cares about grows old and dies.

"Teach me," I say. "And together we'll work wonders."

Maya pulls back a few inches and I see tears on her cheeks.

"Not together, I am afraid."

Something in her voice stops my breath. "What?"

"We will be as one, always, and we will stay here together for a long time while I teach you all I know, but then we must part."

My skin goes cold. "No! What are you saying?"

"Only for a time, Will. We cannot be always together."

"Why not?"

"It is Gaea's way that we separate at times. There are so few of us, and so much to do. Surely you see that. But you will not be losing me, Will. We will always know where the other is, we will always be able to find each other, and when we do it will be as if we were never apart."

Her assurances ease my pain, but only slightly. I feel I'm losing almost as much as I've gained.

"But what about those in-between times?" I say.

"You will be traveling, honing your powers and healing others. Come."

She breaks free, takes my hand, and guides me to the edge of the plateau.

We stand together, looking out over the village and the ocean. It's a new day for us, a new world for me.

"We have work to do and a love to share, you and I," Maya whispers. "And all the time in the world to do it."

Hampton Roads Publishing Company

. . . for the evolving human spirit

Hampton Roads Publishing Company
publishes books on a variety of subjects,
including metaphysics, health,
visionary fiction, and other related topics.

For a copy of our latest catalog, call toll-free
(800) 766-8009, or send your name and address to:

Hampton Roads Publishing Company, Inc.
1125 Stoney Ridge Road
Charlottesville, VA 22902

e-mail: hrpc@hrpub.com
www.hrpub.com